"For ten years Randy Pope has challenged church leaders all over America to adopt an alternative approach to doing church. His insights and application are not theory. Under his leadership, Perimeter Church has successfully duplicated their model in over twenty locations throughout Atlanta. With the creation of *The Prevailing Church*, Randy has made available his timeless insights to pastors everywhere. This book has the potential to transform your leadership as well as your church."

    Andy Stanley
    Senior Pastor, North Point Community Church
    Alpharetta, Georgia

"To those who long for guidance, here are seeds of destiny. What a gift! I wish that every starting and striving pastor I know would plunge into these chapters—they would emerge exhilarated."

    Carl George
    Consulting for Growth, Diamond Bar, California

"I have known Randy Pope for more than twenty years, and what he has written in *The Prevailing Church* is an inviting expression of the passion that is the signature of his life and ministry. . . . In this book, Randy has given the Church a refreshing, creative, biblical approach that rescues us from the rut of just 'doing church.' . . . This book is an invigorating breath of fresh air!"

    Dr. Crawford W. Loritts Jr.
    Speaker, Author, Radio Host
    Associate Director, Campus Crusade for Christ USA

"Wow! A practical and profound book on ministry design that isn't so complicated that only a genius could understand it or so superficial and shallow that nobody would want to. This is a book that ought to be in the hands of every pastor who loves the church and wants to see the church shatter the gates of hell. Randy Pope has been there, done that, and has the T-shirt. If you're a pastor and you miss this one, you ought to go into vinyl repair."

    Steve Brown
    Professor of Preaching at Reformed Theological Seminary
    Bible Teacher, Key Life

"*The Prevailing Church* is not a theoretical book. Randy Pope lives and practices what he preaches. This book should be an inspiration to every church leader who is willing to be open to God's vision."

Dr. Michael Youssef
Founding Rector
The Church of the Apostles

"It is said that 'good fruit' is evidence of a good root. I have seen first-hand the 'fruit' of Randy Pope's ministry in the changed lives of his church members, the healthy growth of his church and the authenticity of his life and leadership. Now Randy desires to help every church and church leader make sure they are having fruit in their own ministry . . . fruit that remains!"

Dr. Bob Reccord
President, Southern Baptist North American Mission Board

"I know of no one better than Randy Pope at thinking strategically about church ministry—and especially about evangelism. His lifelong effectiveness and achievement as the pastor of Perimeter Church and its network attests to this. This book distills Randy's considerable wisdom about these subjects into a very readable volume."

Tim Keller
Senior Pastor, Redeemer Presbyterian Church
New York, New York

"With the experience of a seasoned servant-warrior, the wisdom which can only come with tears and scars, the helpful applications of a faithful practioner, Randy Pope has given us his heart, and not just an outstanding book on the church. Who needs this book? Pastors like me who need to be reminded of the things which mean the most to the heart of God. Congregations like mine, which too easily can become consumer driven, rather than being consumed with the glory and grace of Jesus Christ."

Scotty Smith,
Senior Pastor, Christ Community Church,
Franklin, Tennessee

"I've watched Randy Pope for over twenty years, as he has emerged into ministry beginning with nothing but a devoted wife and commitment to reach a community for Christ. I've seen him innovate, hone and execute multiple strategies, testing them to see which ones stood the test of time. This book is the fruit of that labor. Randy has been used of God to build one of the finest churches in America—a thoughtful, powerful, relational, evangelistic, assimilating, multiplying and kingdom impact church. He shares his strategy in this book with clarity and practical tools for empowerment. Catch his heart and the heart of his church and it will rock your world. May his tribe increase!"

Dr. Ron Jenson
Chairman, Future Achievement International
San Diego, California

"Randy Pope is a man of extraordinary vision for the church. Just being around him awhile you know that he's an extremely gifted leader. It is a blessing for the kingdom that he has used his vision and leadership gifts to have such an impact on Perimeter Church and Perimeter's ministries. His insight will challenge you and stretch your vision. It will help you to dream dreams for your ministry and local church."

G. Bryant Wright
Senior Pastor, Johnson Ferry Baptist Church

"Randy Pope is one of the most gifted and creative ministers I know. For years he has been doing seminars for pastors on how to build a prevailing church. Now he has put his principles in book form making this powerful material available on a broad scale. Here are the principles that have resulted in reaching the unchurched and developing mature, reproducing disciples!"

Frank M. Barker, Jr.
Pastor Emeritus, Briarwood Presbyterian Church
Birmingham, Alabama

"When I'm asked to list significant church leaders in 21st century America, the name Randy Pope is one I always include. With God's blessing, Perimeter has built a church culture that is uniquely equipped to reach people for Christ in our post-modern world. In *The Prevailing Church*, Randy Pope lays out the principles and practicalities that have produced such an effective work for God. If your goal is to build a powerful church for Christ, then this is your book!"

> Lon Solomon
> Senior Pastor, McLean Bible Church
> McLean, Virginia

"I wish I had this book when I began pastoring churches. Congregations, laymen and pastors will profit by examining how Randy Pope implemented biblical principles of developing lay leadership of ministry at all levels of the church. At Perimeter Church, Randy is not a one man gang. Instead he has a large gang of trained lay people doing the work of the ministry."

> Dr. Jim Baird
> Pastor Emeritus, First Presbyterian Church
> Jackson, Mississippi
> Dean of Chapel, Belhaven College
> Director of Church Relations
> Reformed Theological Seminar, Jackson, Mississippi

"If anyone knows how to do church, it's Randy Pope . . . and with excellence! I highly recommend *The Prevailing Church*, a timely and transforming book filled with practical jewels that will enrich every ministry."

> Dr. Robert M. Lewis
> Teaching Pastor, Fellowship Bible Church
> Little Rock, Arkansas

THE
Prevailing Church

An Alternative Approach To Ministry

RANDY POPE

MOODY PRESS
CHICAGO

Moody Press, a ministry of Moody Bible Institute,
is designed for education, evangelization, and edification.
If we may assist you in knowing more about Christ
and the Christian life, please write us without obligation:
Moody Press, c/o MLM, Chicago, Illinois 60610.

Library of Congress Cataloging-in-Publication Data

Pope, Randy.
    The prevailing church: an alternative approach to ministry design / Randy Pope.
    p. cm.
    ISBN 0-8024-2741-3
    1. Pastoral theology. I. Title.

BV4011.3 .P67 2002
253--dc21   2002025050

3 5 7 9 10 8 6 4 2

Printed in the United States of America

Dedicated to my two families who have loved me unconditionally throughout these many years:

Carol, Matt, Rachael, Dena, and David, who have made my personal life a daily joy; and the people of Perimeter Church, who have patiently endured enough mistakes, weaknesses, and failures to eventually emerge as a church which prevails

Contents

Foreword

When Randy Pope asked me to write the foreword to *The Prevailing Church*, I was struck by the thought of how the work he launched in 1977, Perimeter Church, has been just that: *prevailing*.

This book is the story and ministry philosophy of Perimeter Church. Starting with a few dollars and no core group, Randy and his wife, Carol, set out on a journey which has taken them from "victory unto victory" with all the in-between struggles, hurts, and growing pains associated with forward thinking ministries. Through twenty-five years of societal change, economic ups and downs, and spiritual formations, Perimeter Church has been and is, *prevailing*.

Randy Pope is faithful and innovative. In a very quiet and systematic manner, he has lead Perimeter to become a model church in evangelism, discipleship, and leadership development —all of which are very dear to my heart.

Because of Randy's tenacious faithfulness, and others following his example over the years, Perimeter has grown mightily in influence in Atlanta, and beyond. He has led Perimeter in planting over twenty additional churches in the sprawling

Atlanta area with a goal to plant eighty more in the next ten years. Under his leadership, Perimeter has designed a unique approach to Christian schooling, becoming a model to new schools around the country, and has begun church planting centers in nine countries, responsible for planting hundreds of churches internationally.

Few congregations across the country have the benefit of a long-tenured, founding pastor, like Randy, with such a marked passion for the lost. Those who do tend to be *prevailing* churches.

The Prevailing Church is a relevant resource whether you are a pastor or lay person. Within it, you'll find not only the amazing story of an innovative leader and congregation, but more importantly, a design for ministry which models unselfishness, generosity, and passion for people to savingly experience Jesus Christ.

John C. Maxwell
Founder, The INJOY Group

Acknowledgments

Many thanks are in order to my wife, Carol, and our kids for their willingness to give away their husband and dad for two weeks each summer for four years so that I could write this book.

Thank you, Rob Reichel, for securing a spot for me to write in Hilton Head, South Carolina, each of those summers. And a special thanks to Hilton Head residents David and Kathy Brown and Robert and Manelle Graves for allowing me to use their homes when they were gone to do all this writing. I am greatly indebted to Neil Wilson, who did an outstanding job of editing this work, and to my secretary, Jackie Lucas, for the hours she spent preparing my manuscript, getting it ready for the publisher. And speaking of publishers, I am so grateful for the many gracious people I have gotten to know at Moody, especially Jim Bell, Senior Editor, with whom I have worked closely.

And last, but not least, thanks to the staff of Perimeter Church, who labored diligently with me, experimenting with ideas to see what worked; to our elders, who encouraged me to write and have lovingly shepherded me consistently; and to our church members, who have been willing "to attempt things doomed to failure unless God be in them."

May these thoughts and shared experiences, in some small way, benefit the King and His kingdom to whom I owe my all.

To God be the glory.

Introduction

I have intentionally waited toward the end of my first quarter-century of pastoring a church before writing on this subject. And even now, I can't tell you with what tentativeness I write—not because I don't feel strongly about my beliefs, but in fact because I do.

Some of my tentativeness comes as I realize that much of what I say will be limited by my individual experiences and may not easily apply universally. I also know that some of what you will read in these pages, though it is an accurate description of applied biblical principles, will be misunderstood. It breaks too many long-accepted and seldom-questioned "rules" about God's design for the church. I also live with the realization that some of what I practice now as I write will have changed by the time you read this.

I must tell you these things at the outset because the church vision under which I minister, which I call the *prevailing church*, while it has a solid structure and design like a building, is also an organism. It grows, ages, changes, learns, adapts, and continually seeks to become more like what her Lord intends her to be. Yes, many of the details will have been changed by the time you read these words, but the core will remain. I'm convinced you will see this. I'm also convinced that the principles you are about to consider in these pages would definitely look different if applied in the place God has called you to faithfully minister.

This effort also comes out of respect and passion for others God has called into ministry. As I have taught this same content at pastors' conferences and in doctoral studies, I have continually been asked if any of what I teach is in writing. This is my attempt to respond to those requests. In spite of twenty-five years of experience behind them, read these pages as a work in progress.

For well over fifteen years, I have been enamored with the idea of what I have called a "prevailing church." I have taught seminars to pastors for many years under that heading and knew that if I ever wrote on the church, it would be under that title. Several years ago our elders encouraged me to take two weeks a year to write out my convictions and what I had learned regarding church. Five years ago I began this process, writing for two weeks each summer.

Two years into the process, Willow Creek Community Church began advertising its church conference under the same title. Neither of us knew the other was using this title. All this to say that though our churches partner together in numerous ways and my respect for both Bill Hybels and Willow Creek is great, there is no intentional connection in the use of this name. I am glad that the vision for such a church that prevails is being pursued in multiple fashions. My expectation is that both will complement the other in seeing God's kingdom "come to earth, even as it is in heaven."

Through the years I have noticed an interesting phenomenon. The further I get away from the church I pastor in Atlanta, Perimeter Church, the better she looks as a church. When I teach and share about church, illustrated by this church, those who hear me commonly end up viewing Perimeter as a much better church than she really is. Though I always try to communicate honestly, with full integrity, I know wrong assumptions are made. Based on past experiences, those assumptions could leave people thinking that Perimeter is the model church. I love

Perimeter Church as none other, but like a parent with his or her children, I know better than anyone the flaws that exist.

Were you to move to Atlanta and join Perimeter, I would hope and expect that you would love her too. But only then would you see how flawed the ministry is, how many significant weaknesses need to be addressed, and how many opportunities we have to beautify this portion of Christ's bride. And I guess that those opportunities are a big part of what has kept me pastoring this church these many years.

So passion overcomes hesitancy. I have had to write these pages for all the reasons I just gave, and because there is so much ahead. The discipline of putting our experience into written form has been a wonderful way to reflect, identify areas for further attention, and recognize, in circumstances I might have previously overlooked or forgotten, that God has graciously been faithful to His Word repeatedly over the years. I invite you to explore with me a vision of the living, beautiful, powerful, and prevailing church of Jesus Christ.

---◦◦◦◦---

Chapter One

The Church—
Prevailing or Precautious?

Assume you have just moved into a new community and face the task of finding a church. First, you let your fingers do the walking through the yellow pages. Then you look around, call around, and ask around. Eventually, you know you will have to test-drive several churches to find one that seems to fit. What single adjective or descriptive term would you choose to best describe the church for which you would be searching?

- Evangelical
- Bible believing
- Growing
- Friendly
- Family oriented
- Worshipful

Without question, I know the adjective I would choose:

- Prevailing

When I present the ideas you are about to read in seminary classes, church conferences, and pastors' conferences, I find that most in my audience have never even thought of that particular word when they define or describe a healthy church. And yet, as we shall see, it is the term Jesus used to summarize the character of His church. The more I have reflected on and used the word, the more I have come to appreciate the powerful aspects of Jesus' purposes for His people that this particular word conveys.

Dictionaries define the term *prevailing* as meaning "gaining the advantage or mastery, being victorious, effective, lasting, stronger." I use the word *prevailing* to describe a church that conquers in regard to her mission

- to be victorious against spiritual resistance in order to bring a wider community into an encounter with the kingdom of God; and
- to see her people and then her social, moral, political, and educational environments come into greater conformity to the will of God.

I'm convinced that such a church can be identified by her contagious enthusiasm and invigorating vitality. A prevailing church models such a dynamic spirit of worship and servanthood that she becomes a magnet for people needing help. Such a church is a place where insincere people tend to fall away and sincere people long to belong. And, most important, it is a place where nonbelievers find Christ and grow to spiritual maturity. To put it another way, it's a place where the presence of God's power is demonstrated with such force that the community in which it exists is marked with an indelible spiritual imprint.

CONTRAST

From my early childhood, I experienced growing up in a church that was everything but prevailing. That church, and many like it that I have since observed, was not only on the other side of the continuum from a prevailing church but was even headed in a different direction. In fact, I now call a church like my childhood church a precautious church.

The term *precautious* means "taking necessary measure against possible danger, harm or failure." My childhood church knew nothing about taking risks and a lot about minimal survival. It maintained a meager existence free from controversy primarily because it stood for everything. One could be a member and believe and act any way he or she pleased. In exchange for demanding practically no real commitment from her members, my childhood church offered little of lasting spiritual value.

The precautious church is free from failure only because of its unwillingness to attempt great accomplishments for the sake of God and His kingdom. In times that require boldness, a precautious church is afraid of its own shadow. Such a church lives by the unspoken motto, "We've Got Everything to Lose and Nothing to Gain."

A precautious church is one best described by terms such as

- Lifeless
- Powerless
- Visionless
- Defeated

ANTI-HERO

As a child, I was heard to say at least once, "I don't know what I'll do when I grow up, but one thing I know for sure I'll never be." You guessed it! A preacher.

I had not yet seen anything in the church that could capture my passion. Nor had I met a pastor I saw as a man's man. Had I met such a man, I would have seriously questioned why he would give himself to such a feeble cause.

Fortunately, God didn't leave me with such limited experience. Jesus Christ proved more attractive than His representatives in my life. I eventually became a follower of Christ. Then, early in my spiritual pilgrimage as a new believer, I was introduced to churches that shattered my previous idea of the body of Christ. Those congregations had qualities I now call *prevailing* and leaders I now call *visionary*—and I fell in love with God's church.

WHAT WAS DIFFERENT?

In those churches I met people who saw themselves, not as a precautious service organization, but as a wartime army engaged in battle. Within their often ordinary lives they displayed a remarkable sense of purpose. They were serious about their faith without taking on self-righteous airs. They were comfortable with spiritual warfare terminology without casting themselves as the heroes in God's work. They were convinced that there was too much to gain in God's service to worry about possible losses. They were more concerned about following the Lord than about what it might cost along the way. Their attitude was contagious! I determined then that only a prevailing church would be worthy of my full devotion.

THE BIBLICAL PICTURE

So that we can get a clearer picture of the prevailing church, let's look at the context in which Jesus used the term to describe the church. Jesus called His church *prevailing* during an episode in His early ministry, described in the sixteenth chapter of Matthew's gospel.

Jesus had taken His small band of followers into the district known as Caesarea Philippi. Perhaps while looking at the various shrines built on the nearby hillside to honor man-made gods, Jesus began to talk about public opinion. He may have first pointed to some of those idols and asked, "What do people really think about these gods?" That question would have certainly set the stage for what followed.

We join the discussion in time to hear Jesus ask the disciples, "Who do people say that the Son of Man is?" (Matthew 16:13). The disciples' response was interesting in that every name they mentioned identified Jesus as someone returned from the dead: "Some say John the Baptist; and others, Elijah; but still others, Jeremiah, or one of the prophets" (v. 14).

Apparently, people in general recognized the supernatural aspects of Christ's life and ministry, but they grossly erred in their opinions about His identity. Their guesses seem closer to tabloid headlines than the truth. In spite of abundant hints from Scripture, the people suffered from category limitations. They missed and, in some cases, studiously ignored the obvious.

EVERY PREVAILING CHURCH IS AN ORIGINAL.

Yet Jesus was not particularly concerned about the errant observations of the masses. His question was a warm-up volley. Neither His identity nor His plan depended on public opinion polls. Jesus didn't intend to build His church and ultimately conquer the world for His kingdom's cause through ill-informed crowds. He would do so through men and women just like His first twelve.

So now, Jesus served up the significant question: "But who do you say that I am?" (v. 15). Peter, the unofficial and self-appointed leader of the disciples, was quick, as usual, to respond: "You are the Christ, the Son of the living God." (v. 16). His impulsive exclamation could not have been more precise or accurate. For once, Peter actually blurted out the truth!

Jesus let Peter know how blessed he was to be so accurate, making sure he also knew that only God the Father deserved the credit for giving him such insight and understanding (v. 17). Peter was probably nod-ding his head in agreement at these words when Jesus continued. What came next must have caught Peter completely off guard. Jesus certainly captured his heart with a vision he would remember every time he heard his name: "I also say to you that you are Peter, and upon this rock I will build My church; and the gates of Hades will not overpower [or prevail against] it" (v. 18).

FLASH-FORWARD

Jesus' simple statement has brought forth a greater diversity of in-terpretation than almost any text in Scripture—and created profound implications for the church throughout her history. Every church today must in some way see her existence as a result of these words of Jesus.

The major division in Western Christianity illustrates the widest gap between the understandings of Jesus' statement. On one side, the Roman church equates the name *Peter* (*Petra*) to the term *rock* (*petros*) in the verse, concluding that Jesus then declared Peter to be the appointed authority of the church to be handed down to succeeding leaders known as popes.

On the other side, Protestants, highlighting the distinction between a small stone (*petra*) and a large rock or boulder (*petros*), believe Jesus was stating that the church would be built on something far more sub-stantial than one "infallible" individual. Some holding this view sug-gest that the foundation of His church will be the same confession uttered by Peter, that Christ is the Son of the living God. Others believe that the rock refers to followers who, like Peter, hold such a confession. Still others conclude that Jesus meant that He would build His church on Himself, the true Rock and foundation of the church.

Regardless of one's perspective, all three Protestant views lead to the same conclusion and, I'm convinced, the correct biblical teaching of the text. The confession itself, those making the confession, and the Christ of the confession Himself are all ingredients of a church that will be so potent that the gates of hades shall not prevail against it.

BACK TO THE BEGINNING

Assume again that you are still a recent arrival, looking for a church. Have you changed your mind in any way about the kind of church you are seeking? If I have done my job in this first chapter, I have at least piqued your curiosity to find out more about this idea of a prevailing church. I am amazed how seldom church leaders think seriously about the way their church presents herself to strangers. Yet, unless a church can honestly assess her appearance and clearly identify her specific purposes for existing, she is likely to lack a number of important traits. She is also not likely to prevail.

I fully realize that you may be reading this as a highly motivated young pastor or a veteran in ministry. I hope your curiosity has been stirred also. In the last few years I have heard from a growing number who are confused and overwhelmed by pre-prepackaged church models. Others are tired of trying various ministry structures, disillusioned with one model after another that doesn't seem to work in their setting, no matter how hard they try. Let me both warn and encourage you: the prevailing church is neither a package nor a model. Every prevailing church is an original.

We usually apply Ephesians 2:8–10 to God's purpose in the life of an individual. It can also be applied to a church: "For it is by grace you have been saved, through faith—and this not from yourselves, it is the gift of God—not by works, so that no one can boast. For we are God's workmanship, created in Christ Jesus to do good works, which God prepared in advance for us to do" (NIV). Wouldn't a church which clearly saw herself this way tend to prevail?

So this book is not going to offer you another mold into which you can try to squeeze your church. The prevailing church vision has a lot to do with development and long-term perspective. The prevailing church vision has even more to do with the workmanship Jesus Christ wants to accomplish with His church in a specific place. The prevailing church, instead of being a mold, often breaks molds. Yes, there are some underlying patterns and consistent structural elements. Jesus does have a certain style. You will recognize the characteristics in the next few chapters. I expect that many of them are already present in the church you call your spiritual home. My purpose is to help you check all the biblical character traits that have been lived out in prevailing churches throughout history in the hopes that you will consider giving attention to any that might be missing in your church.

As I tried to make clear in the Introduction, I don't consider Perimeter Church to be the perfect example of a prevailing church. She is simply the example I know best. Nor do I consider the two extremes of *prevailing* and *precautious* to be hardened categories that perfectly describe every church as one or the other. The terms are better used to describe underlying intentions and directions. This translates into the question, "Is our church consciously seeking to be prevailing?"

My prayer behind every page of this book is that God might use it to help awaken Christ's church to the thrilling adventure of prevailing! Jesus made clear that His church is to prevail. I am convinced that one of the healthiest questions a church leadership team can regularly ask themselves is, "In how many ways are we living like a prevailing church?"

Chapter Two

Four Marks of
a Prevailing Church

In order to establish a foundation for understanding the prevailing church vision, allow me to suggest four marks, or general characteristics, of such a church. These can easily serve as a diagnostic tool to evaluate the degree to which individual believers and congregations are, in reality, prevailing. The four basic character traits come directly from the interaction Jesus had with His disciples in which He claimed that His church would prevail against what He called the "gates of Hades" (Matthew 16:18).

THE PREVAILING CHURCH

1. *The prevailing church is composed of people who live out the confession that Christ is Lord.*

It should come as no surprise that Jesus continued in the same context and setting of Peter's confession and His own self-revelation by introducing the requirements for being His disciple. In Matthew 16:24–25(NASB 1977), we read: "Then Jesus said to His disciples, 'If anyone wishes to come after Me, let him deny himself, and take up his cross, and follow Me. For whoever wishes to save his life shall lose it; but whoever loses his life for My sake shall find it.'"

HOW THE CHURCH SEES HERSELF
AFFECTS HOW SHE ACTS IN THE WORLD.

The standards upon which Jesus decided to build His church have never had any room for selective obedience. But you wouldn't arrive at that conclusion looking at many Christians today. A professing follower of Christ is asked if he steals. His answer? "Absolutely not." When asked, "Why?" his response is, "I'm a Christian, and God says not to steal." He is then asked, "Have you ever taken someone's life?" Once again, for the same reason he says, "Never." But when asked, as a single thirty-year-old, if he observes sexual abstinence, his response is often a slow and sheepish, "Well, I guess not as much as I should." Does God's Word equally forbid sexual promiscuity as it does stealing or murder? Absolutely, but today it seems to be in vogue among many Christians to observe a mutated form of Christianity whose central belief turns out to be what I call "selective obedience."

I fully realize that such specific challenges are often met with the concern that Christians must not be legalistic. We are certainly not to select a list of standards we can use to point out the flaws in other Christians' lives. My response to the concern over legalism is to point out that our alternative has almost eliminated our capacity to clearly represent Christ in the world. Whether we look at divorce statistics or other behavioral factors, those who claim to be Christians are looking more and more like the world instead of being salt or light. Yes, Christians fail. But I have far more hope for the effectiveness of a Christian who fails while genuinely trying to be wholeheartedly obedient to Christ than for the Christian who selects a few ways in which he or she will exhibit obedience (and often ends up failing at even those). Christianity with low or no expectations is the Christianity of the precautious church.

Such thinking was certainly not part of our Lord's prescription for the believers who would constitute the prevailing church. He fully and clearly expected His followers to be people who would deny themselves and take up their cross (die to their own desires and pleasures) and follow Him (His example and the teaching of His written Word). That is why Jesus elsewhere (Luke 14:25–35) actually discouraged eager people from becoming disciples until they had seriously counted the cost that would be involved in following Him!

So the first characteristic of the prevailing church is that it is composed of people who faithfully live out their confession that Christ is Lord, particularly in the areas of obedience that may be under assault at any moment in history. To this first descriptive statement we must add further clarifying statements.

2. *The prevailing church is composed of people who live out their confession within the shadows of the gates of hades.*

Jesus' definition of the prevailing church included several familiar images from His times—warfare, defeat, gates, and prevailing. He lived among people chaffing under Roman occupation. Jesus continually pointed out that His purposes, though falling into the category of warfare, had little or nothing to do with the Roman powers. People expected the Messiah to overthrow the current *earthly* enemy; Jesus intended to defeat their *spiritual* foe. The Jews wanted to prevail against *Rome;* Jesus wanted His followers to prevail against *hell.*

In ancient Eastern cultures, the meeting place for the community's authority or ruling body was often at the front gates of the city. Long before city halls there were city gates. These gates were much more than passages. They represented access, safety, defense, and vulnerability. A fortified city was only as strong as its gates. The term *hades* is literally *to see* prefixed by *not.* Thus, it refers to the unseen, or spiritual world. When

Jesus used the phrase "gates of Hades" in Matthew 16:18, He was referring to the spiritual stronghold from which Satan and his legions storm
out into the world with the assignment and intention of deceiving the
lost, destroying the witness of the church, and controlling society.

Notice, however, the picture Jesus actually presented in His statement. The gates are a fixed place. They withstand or splinter under the
pounding of the battering ram. Jesus was describing a city under assault.
He foresaw His church attacking and laying siege to Satan's stronghold.
He promised that He and His church would eventually breach the gates
of hell. So why is it that our teaching about the reality of spiritual warfare too often pictures the church under siege rather than the church ar-
rayed and battering down the defenses of Satan? Why do we see ourselves
in a defensive posture, holding out under attack rather than an army in
full counterattack mode? As long as we accept that precarious, hunkered-
down-behind-the-walls description of the church, we allow Satan to keep
the gates of hades wide open and in full operation in this world!

Mental imagery makes a difference. How the church sees herself af-
fects how she acts in the world. Perhaps recent events in our country will
make military object lessons acceptable once again. They are certainly
an integral part of the biblical teaching. My intention in using militaristic
language has nothing to do with my desire to glorify the dangers and
difficulties of the Christian life and everything to do with my desire to
honor and clarify what Jesus told His disciples about His church and
her opposition in the world. The same teacher who promised His followers that they would become fishers of men also promised His followers
that they would prevail against the gates of hades.

These open gates of hades are blatantly evident within the structures
of today's society. It takes only a quick glimpse into the school systems
of today to see the evidence of the control and influence of the gates of
hades. Several years ago, a high school student who grew up in our church
was suspended from school for merely handing a friend a written announcement of an evening Fellowship of Christian Athletes meeting
to be held that night at his home. The note was passed between classes,
in a hallway. A watching hall monitor confiscated the note and sent

the student to the principal's office. There he received the sentence for his crime—suspension from school.

Without question, the gates of hades are evident today in not only our schools but also in our social clubs, neighborhood gatherings, medical societies, libraries, judicial court systems, and political parties. The gates of hades are regretfully found even amidst many of the churches of today. Satan's power has not increased; Christ's church has simply failed in large numbers to take her role seriously. Believers have left the field of battle in droves. Our view of ourselves as soldiers has become passé or ignored. I wouldn't say the precautious church is losing; I would say this kind of church isn't even seriously trying!

In fact, the gates of hades are prevailing almost unchallenged in the lost world. They must be confronted by believers who will live out their confession within the shadows, laying siege to the gates of hades. The precautious church is certainly no threat to the unseen authorities; in fact, she has become an aid and ally to them by her silence and lethargy. The precautious church has a victim mentality, unable or unwilling to take up the offensive. The world is waiting, and the gates of hades are daring the church to be the church!

3. *The prevailing church accepts its commission to take up the battle for the souls of lost people.*

To put this characteristic another way, we can say that a prevailing church is committed equally to the task of "mission" as it is to the task of "home." I am using the term *mission* here as a term to describe the church's commitment to reaching the lost, and the term *home* to refer to its task to care for, feed, and protect God's people. (The term *mission* is also used in this book in the sense of ministry plan; see especially chapter 9). It is disappointing, to say the least, to see how few churches feel, teach, or carry out a passion for the lost. They may talk "mission," but we don't see them walk "mission." I am convinced that unless the dual roles of mission and home are equally understood and practiced in the local church the outcome will be a failure to prevail.

While on a study leave one summer several years ago, I was evaluating our church and my role as its leader. Throughout those days, I was spending time devotionally in Luke 15. This is the passage in which Jesus relates the stories of the lost sheep, the lost coin, and the lost son. During one of my meditation times, I focused on the parable of the lost sheep. If you remember, one sheep, out of a flock of one hundred, went astray. The shepherd immediately left the ninety-nine to search for the one lost.

Keep in mind that sheep feel very insecure when their shepherd is not present and available. In other words, in this story, we have ninety-nine very dissatisfied sheep. Meanwhile, the shepherd, upon finding the one lost sheep, hoisted it on his shoulder and came home rejoicing. Then we read Jesus' pointed and profound application of the story: "I tell you that in the same way, there will be more joy in heaven over one sinner who repents, than over ninety-nine righteous persons who need no repentance" (Luke 15:7 NASB 1977).

Conviction

I am convinced that a majority of the best church members, at least in this nation, do not believe this text. In fact, if you were to disguise this truth and present it without identifying its origin in God's Word, the majority of Christians would reject this teaching as illogical and not representing the values of God.

As I pondered this passage, I wrote the following words in my journal:

> The passion of Christ and His Father is to reach a lost world. For a pastor to embrace this same passion is to make him appear suspect in the best of evangelical churches.

When I share this conviction around the country at pastors' conferences, I find unanimous agreement and identification with this statement. After all, it is "shallow teaching" that reaches the lost, while mature believers need the "deeper truths" that they hire pastors to deliver. And who's for being shallow instead of deep?

I went on:

It's unacceptable to leave the ninety-nine to look for the lost. Church members are very forbearing and forgiving regarding the neglect of the lost; while extremely impatient and unforgiving regarding the neglect of the righteous.

Think of a continuum on which the left end represents an extremely effective "home" function of a church, and the right end represents an extremely effective "mission" function.

After journaling these thoughts, I decided to evaluate the church I pastor in light of this continuum. Believing a healthy and balanced church would find its X placed in the center, I had to honestly admit that our X was placed well left of center—being far more effective as a home to God's people than as a mission to the unchurched.

Lessons from the Flock

Through the years, we have had numerous people leave our church feeling that their needs as believers had not been met, and frankly, many of them had legitimate complaints. Yet what grieves me the most is that never during those years has anyone so much as complained about our ineffectiveness as a mission. Many have left for personal reasons; none have departed because we failed to care for the lost. When have you ever lost a member because your church was failing to effectively reach the lost?

I left my study leave with that convicting evaluation on my heart. I made the commitment to give my best to leading our church in such a way as to find that X placed on the continuum where it needed to be.

That commitment to intentional mission has met its share of challenges. They often come unexpectedly. Here's a good example. I received a phone call from a man out of state whom I had never met. He explained that he was moving his family to Atlanta and that his work would allow him to live anywhere he chose in the city. He had decided to make that decision based on his choice of church. Because time did not allow him to visit churches in Atlanta, he was doing his "church shopping" over the phone. He proceeded to make the following statement and then ask a question. He said, "I have heard that your church is highly committed to reaching the unchurched." He then added, "Don't get me wrong. I am too." Can you guess his next word? You got it! "But," he said, "I need to know if the church's commitment to reach the unchurched could in any way hinder my needs or the needs of my family from being met?"

I was grieved by the mere question. After a lengthy pause, I finally responded by saying, "No, but it is my greatest ambition that one day soon the entire church and its resources will be so given to reaching the unchurched that it could at least be perceived that the believers' needs were being neglected" (though the two are really not at odds with one another, as will be explained later).

The Balance

The truth is that the greatest way to neglect the needs of God's people is to put them in a church that fails to function as a "mission." The healthiest environment for nurture and discipleship is that of "mission." Otherwise, nurture and discipleship become ends rather than means to accomplish God's greater purposes. Unless the twin priorities of "home" and "mission" receive appropriate attention, the church functions without a healthy balance.

I have learned through years of discipling men that I can teach them the truths and commitments of our faith without seeing any automatic by-product of zeal for mission. When I put them in an environment of mission, however, I find them to be hungry and anxious to be fed and nurtured. Much in the way that eating creates no appetite for exercise, so too I have found that Bible study and prayer alone do not create mission-oriented Christians. But, just as exercise creates a desire for food and drink, mission-related activities create an insatiable thirst and hunger to feed on God's Word.

People have asked through the years what accounts for God's great blessing on Perimeter Church. I certainly answer by pointing gratefully to God's grace. Then I add that I often imagine God is in the heavens saying to His angels as they prepare to deliver blessing to many of Christ's local churches around the world, "And keep showering Perimeter. They aren't nearly as effective as they should be, but boy, do they have a passion and commitment to reach the unchurched."

So, the prevailing church accepts the commission to take on the battle for the souls of lost people. It carries a passion for the lost. It finds ways to reach unreached people. It is supernaturally orchestrated to the end of reaching lost people. And it is greatly disappointed and frustrated until lost people are being won to God's kingdom.

4. *The prevailing church wins the battle against the gates of hades.*

Certainly the ultimate war between God's church and the powers of the unseen world is settled—and the declared victor will be Christ and His church. Jesus has once and forever sealed the defeat of the Evil One by His death and resurrection and has described in His infallible Word the very details of the final battle of this war.

Yet between now and then, God has abundantly provided His church with power to win the daily skirmishes. He has commissioned His church to fight and has promised her power so as to guarantee victory. But the church must be a people who don't compromise their confession and who, walking right into the very shadows of hades' gates, engage the enemy in the battle for the souls of lost people.

Certainly, the church will have its struggles. Apparent failures will come. But the church has been declared by her Owner and Commander in Chief to be so potent that even the gates of hades can't stand up against her. God's church can, should, and ultimately will be victorious. Within any fertile field, God's church will see large numbers of lost people won to Christ and healthily integrated into the family of God. Through the prevailing church, God's kingdom comes and His will is done on earth.

REFLECTION

Are you ready for your own diagnostic evaluation? The questions you are about to look at are difficult to answer. They expose shortcomings. They continually humble me. But I keep coming back to them because I realize that unless I have a clear picture of my present state, I will not know where to start in order to keep moving in the right direction. Put simply, how would you answer the following questions applied to you individually or to the collective body of your church?

1. *To what extent do you (or your church membership at large) live out the confession that Christ is Lord?*

Are you struggling with selective obedience? In what ways do you tend to compromise your convictions in light of personal pleasure or peer pressure?

2. *To what extent do you (or your church membership at large) live out your confession within the shadows of the gates of hades?*

How many non-Christians do you know well and would they know that your greatest commitment and allegiance is to Christ? In what segments of society have you planted yourself as one who holds the confession of Christ as Son of the living God?

3. *In what specific ways have you (or your church membership at large) taken on the battle for the souls of the lost people?*

Whether it is your neighborhood, your marketplace, or your civic or social club, have you identified your target group? To do so is to enhance the likelihood of effectively battling for the souls of lost people. If you were asked, "What is your target group for reaching people for Christ?" how quickly and clearly would you respond? If you are slow to answer, it probably suggests that you are not as effective at reaching the lost as you could be.

The last diagnostic question is perhaps the most revealing of all.

4. Are you (or your church membership at large) winning the battle against the gates of hades?

The victory in this battle is determined by obedience. Obedience includes not simply doing the right things, but doing the right things for the right reasons and in the power of God's indwelling Spirit. This obedience may be in any area of life, but one often-neglected command involves our role in winning the lost world. When God's church prevails, new believers enter God's kingdom. Some will see thirtyfold, some sixty and some one hundred. But lives change when God's church prevails. Can you identify people this past year who have come into God's kingdom at least in part because of the influence of your life or the message you have declared? Has your church grown by adding brand-new Christians who are professing for the first time that Christ is now their Master? If so, there's evidence that God's church is prevailing against the gates of hades.

I realize that I have focused almost exclusively on the impact of a prevailing church upon the unchurched. But certainly the gates of hades must be confronted in the minds and hearts of believers as well. Regardless, the foundation for every victory is Christ—thus the centrality of the confession that Christ is the Son of the living God. It is in Him and in Him alone that victory is secured.

Before moving on to a treatment plan, we must consider a summary diagnostic question: Would your life (or your church) most accurately be described by the word *prevailing* or the word *precautious?* Remember that my concern behind this question has to do with direction. Which of the terms expresses the direction in which your church is moving? Your honest answer will greatly affect your ability to benefit from the remainder of this book. The next chapter will begin to examine in greater detail the profile of a prevailing church.

———∞∞∞———

Chapter Three

What Makes a Church Grow?

SIX WIDELY RECOGNIZED CAUSES AND AN OFTEN OVERLOOKED SEVENTH FACTOR

What causes a church to grow? In one sense, the answer is quite simple. Paul clearly identified the One who causes growth to be God Himself. In fact, he made it clear that "neither the one who plants nor the one who waters is anything, but God who causes the growth" (1 Corinthians 3:7).

In another sense, however, the answer to the question of what makes a church grow can be quite complex. The underlying divine cause may be clear, but the means God uses may vary greatly. We have to admit that skill sets and leadership gifts, facilities and budgets, along with church-growth principles and programs, all contribute to the equation that results in a unique local church.

The analogy of gardening introduced by Paul in his writing to the church of Corinth (1 Corinthians 3:1–9) is an excellent one for helping us understand church growth. Tim Keller, in an unpublished essay on breaking growth barriers, wrote:

The results of gardening depend on two sets of factors. First, there are the acts of gardening themselves—seeding, watering, weeding, pruning, fertilizing, spraying, etc. Over these factors, the gardener has control. They are a matter of diligence and skill and gift. "I planted the seed, Apollos watered it . . ." (vs. 6). Secondly, there are the contextual factors—the quality of the seed, the weather conditions and the general conditions of the soil. Over these factors, the gardener has no control. They are matters in God's hands. ". . . but God made it grow . . ." (vs. 7). The power of growth is in the seed. The magnitude of growth is heavily dependent on weather conditions and soil conditions. Yet skillful gardening releases the power of the seed. So we can conclude—if we apply sound gardening principles, there will ordinarily be church growth of quantity and quality. But the amount and magnitude of the growth depends on God's "weather condition" and "soil receptivity"—matters out of your hands. . . . If there is little or no growth, it could be due to weather conditions, but we should first look at the quality of the gardening, so as not to shift blame too quickly!

What factors comprise the quality of the gardening? I suggest seven primary factors are critical for healthy church growth (several of which are factors more or less important depending upon the culture in which the church exists). As noted above, six of these are widely accepted, even if they are not very faithfully practiced. The seventh factor describes an overlooked component in church growth. The seventh factor is crucial to the development of a prevailing church. In order for the garden to be healthy and productive over a long period, the seventh factor must be in place.

Let's briefly look at each of the factors.

1. A BIBLICAL THEOLOGY AND POLITY

"You will know the truth, and the truth will make you free" (John 8:32). Churches that long to glorify God and to proclaim Christ will have their differences regarding theology and polity (church government). No one has a corner on the truth so as to interpret God's Word infallibly. It is safe to say, however, that every text of Scripture has only one truthful interpretation, though allowing numerous reasonable and appropriate applications.

Whether it be a proper understanding of law and grace, the meaning of the gospel as applied to seekers and believers alike, or the relationship between the old and new covenant, a church's theological framework and doctrinal beliefs are critical factors regarding its growth. Leadership structure, roles and responsibilities, and one's understanding of authority within the church are going to play a significant role in the growth of a church as well. This is not to say that churches with weak theology and unhealthy polity can't grow. Yet they rarely do and never grow in a healthy way.

SPIRITUAL RENEWAL DYNAMICS REFER TO A WAY OF LIFE THAT IS BOTH GOD-HONORING AND GOD-BLESSED.

Another way to describe this is to relate back to the precarious church. Precarious churches, by definition, rarely get planted or started. That would be entirely too risky! Precarious churches are frequently more like parasites or cancer. Some remain in existence by feeding off the life that was once there. When dysfunctional churches with weak theology do experience growth, it is usually temporary and related to population shifts, a charismatic leader, or even the intentional or accidental impression given to newcomers that the church actually does have a biblical theology and polity. As with the human body, so the church body can experience healthy as well as unhealthy growth. The point remains. The church that consistently embraces the most accurate biblical theology and polity eliminates, in the arena of this first factor, unnecessary obstacles to healthy church growth.

2. SPIRITUAL RENEWAL DYNAMICS

There is no more important ingredient to church growth than the presence of spiritual renewal dynamics. Take away this factor and you have taken out the heart of the church—spiritual life cannot exist without it. Clearly, "unless the LORD builds the house, they labor in vain who build it" (Psalm 127:1).

Spiritual renewal dynamics refer to a way of life that is both God-honoring and God-blessed. It describes the activities of hearts that are yielded to Christ and devoted to His kingdom. It is that which is both the fruit of God's work of grace and its means.

When we think of spiritual renewal dynamics, we immediately think of the faithful and clear proclamation of God's Word and the rightful administration of the Lord's Supper and Baptism. Where this dynamic exists there is a clear understanding and embracing of the gospel—a Christian pilgrimage that begins and ends with grace and finds the keeping of God's law as the fruit of that grace. The gospel is seen as not just a plan of salvation for the lost but a way of life for the believer.

Alongside the proper use of the Scriptures and participation in Baptism and the Lord's Supper must also stand effective prayer and fasting. We talk much of prayer today while saying little about fasting. Vital and continuous spiritual renewal requires prayer with fasting. In such an environment one will typically find in the church humility of heart, repentance, obedience (the nonselective variety), and evangelistic zeal and witness. These dynamics also signal the practice of other healthy spiritual disciplines (Bible study, biblical meditation, simplicity, submission). Each of these dynamics is assumed to be exhibited by believers who have learned to be filled with God's Spirit and who walk in the Spirit on a daily basis.

Add these and other spiritual renewal dynamics to a biblical theology and polity and you have the necessary foundation for the church we are calling the prevailing church.

3. SPIRITUAL, DISCERNING, AND GIFTED LEADERSHIP

Leaders, by definition, lead, not just to the accomplishment of tasks, but most important, to a way of life. Holiness of life and obedience in kingdom service are best taught by modeling. Give to a church spiritual, discerning, and gifted leadership who practice what they preach, and watch the congregation follow.

Most churches today are composed of people who are not deep personal worshipers. I believe the primary reason for this malaise is that so few pastors and elders set the pace or illustrate how to practice worship. How many churches are you aware of where a large percentage of the members are discipling younger believers? I would imagine that the answer is, "Few, at best." But we shouldn't be surprised. Think how few pastors and elders are giving significant time each week to discipling a handful of believers. We can certainly say the same about personal evangelism. At any given pastors' conference, ask how many pastors have personally led someone to Christ in the past year (outside of the means of public preaching). I have found the number to be shockingly few. Ask the same question to the elders of the best of evangelical churches, and I believe it is safe to conclude that the answer will be equally small.

Entirely too many church leaders are expecting their congregations to respond to the general admonition, "Do as I say, not as I do." Entirely too many believers are doing exactly as their leaders do.

4. SPIRITUAL AND MINISTRY-ORIENTED LAITY

All of us who are pastors are guilty at one time or another of complaining about our jobs. Surely, many of those complaints are well-founded. But one does not stand up to scrutiny. It is the complaint of having bad, unleadable, unwilling-to-serve laity. Certainly every church does have its few, but for the most part, church members go where they are led. They grow up as strong as the environment in which they are placed.

My undergraduate work was at the University of Alabama during the days of Alabama football coach Paul "Bear" Bryant. I was an ardent student of him as a leader. Rarely have I observed anyone with greater strength in leadership abilities, and his understanding of leadership seemed to match his abilities.

On one occasion near the end of his extremely successful career, he read in *The Atlanta Journal-Constitution* a quote from the Georgia Tech football coach, Bill Curry. Curry was in the midst of a terrible season and had lost the game on the previous day. He was interviewed by the media, and he refused to take responsibility for the loss. He explained that he had taken responsibility for losing all year but not now. His explanation was that he and his coaches had done their jobs and that on this particular week the players just didn't have the heart and will to win.

During a speech after this episode, Bill Curry told the story of receiving a phone call on that following Monday morning. It was from Bear Bryant. Coach Bryant talked to Curry as a coach would talk to an inattentive player or a father would address his son. He said, "Bill, I read your statement after Saturday's game about not taking responsibility for this loss. I don't ever want to hear such a comment from you ever again. Never forget, you are the leader. You recruited these players. You coach these players. You are the one who must motivate these players. When you lose, you take responsibility for the loss. And, oh, by the way, when you win, you give the boys the credit."

Not long ago I found a widely attributed quote from "The Bear." It says the same thing.

A WORD FROM THE COACH

I'm just a plow hand from Arkansas, but I've learned how to hold a team together, how to lift up some men, how to calm down others, until finally they've got one heartbeat together, a team. There are just three things I'd ever say:

If anything goes bad, I did it.

If anything goes semi-good, then we did it.

If anything goes good, then you did it.

That's all it takes to get people to win football games for you.

A proper understanding of leadership includes knowing where to place responsibility for failure, whether the context is a football team or the church. Without question, spiritual and ministry-oriented laity are prerequisites for a healthy and vibrant church. And it takes time to see such laity developed. But given the right input, time, and environment, strong, committed believers begin to surface.

5. ADEQUATE PROPERTY, FACILITIES, AND PARKING

This fifth factor is one that I had in mind when mentioning that some of these factors vary in importance based on the culture in which the church exists. It would appear to me, based on observation only and without research to support my conclusion, that property, facilities, and parking become a more significant factor the more affluent the society. Regardless of the sociological or economic status, however, property, facilities, and parking most definitely play a critical role in the growth history of many churches.

THE PREVAILING CHURCH IS NOT JUST A CHURCH THAT GROWS; IT IS A CHURCH THAT LASTS!

The church I have been privileged to pastor the past twenty-five years has had facilities in five different locations over these years. Each new home had larger buildings and more parking. And, following each move, we experienced significant new growth. There is certainly a connection.

Building programs and relocation endeavors are dreaded experiences for most pastors. Both are breeding grounds for misunderstanding and division. In an effort to avoid disappointment and controversy, many church leaders actually avoid expansion and relocation efforts. Unfortunately, as these churches try to avoid tension and controversy, they also forfeit the potential of reaching new people because of space limitations.

6. ADEQUATE FINANCIAL RESOURCES

Dr. Howard Hendricks, noted professor at Dallas Theological Seminary, once surprised his students by telling them that one of his greatest concerns for them in future ministry was that they wouldn't have the financial resources necessary to do the work that God would call them to.

Almost everyone in occupational ministry has at one time or another heard the statement that when God calls you to ministry, He supplies the financial resources. True as this may be, it is common to see faithful believers accept God's call into the ministry and then seem to be handcuffed because of limited financial resources. Certainly God is faithful to each of these ministries. The explanation for limited resources is accounted for by numerous reasons. Inadequate education on stewardship, inappropriate and unwise fund-raising techniques, prayerlessness, and risk-avoidance are only a few. Ministries often "have not" because they "ask not." And many ministries that do ask, "have not" because they ask in the wrong way or ask with wrong motives, wishing to spend their resources for their own pleasure (see James 4:3).

Financial resources follow clearly defined vision. The vision must present an objective worthy of sacrificial investment because it is believed to be attainable. In other words, show me a church with a clearly defined vision as well as both a commitment and a plan to accomplish the vision, and I'll show you a church that most likely will have adequate financial resources.

7. AN EFFECTIVE MINISTRY PLAN

What I now introduce is the last of seven factors required for healthy church growth. In my opinion, it is the most often overlooked factor when assessing the cause of church stagnation or decline. It is the most complex of the seven factors and entails a vast variety of important subjects. It could perhaps be best referred to as an effective ministry plan.

As important as the first six factors may be, they can, to a great degree, be neutralized by the failure to have such a plan. Taken alone, the first six factors can certainly contribute to the start of wonderful ministries and explosive churches. But we are targeting a different end and a much longer-term vision. The prevailing church is not just a church that grows; it is a church that lasts! The first six factors, crucial as they are, will not have a long-term impact without an effective ministry plan.

A ministry plan consists of a clearly defined vision and mission with values and is supported by a biblically sound and culturally relevant philosophy of ministry. It includes a strategically designed infrastructure and has well-documented job descriptions and goals. In addition to all this, it has both a commitment and a strategy to successfully accomplish its vision and mission.

Effective ministry plan development forces the church to deal with the many functions of its life that rarely align with one another and often seem to function at far less than peak efficiency. These functions include:

- Leadership development
- Teaching and preaching of God's Word
- Discipleship
- Evangelism
- Church transitions
- Assimilation of new people
- Caring for God's people

This book is actually about this often overlooked and very little understood seventh factor, an effective ministry plan.

THE QUEST

For many years, I have taken several weeks in the summer for personal planning, extended prayer, and ministry evaluation. Several years ago while on this summer leave, I came to the disappointing realization that what I had dreamed about in church ministry would most likely never come to reality.

My hope of seeing the majority of church members becoming mature and equipped followers of Christ was dimming. From my perspective, the development of such disciples on the one hand and the process of church as we know it today on the other were quite incompatible. The processes in place in the church were not actually attaining the expected product of the church—mature and equipped believers. Integrity demanded a change in the expected product or in the existing process.

When I returned home and shared my conclusions with the elders in our church, we had an interesting discussion. They asked if I thought a process existed that could produce such a product. Deep down inside I couldn't help but believe there must be one. But what that way was, I was uncertain. We had already worked for years to build a church. Perimeter was seen by many to be a leader in the process of making mature and equipped followers of Christ. Many people were being won to Christ, small group ministry was thriving, and church growth was constant. Yet we all knew that the potential of the church was far greater than the product being produced.

Our elders commissioned me to take whatever time necessary to discover and return with a plan that I believed could bring the process and the product into alignment. I immediately became a diligent student of the process of developing such a ministry plan. We invested a full year of praying and strategizing as we developed a new plan. Having had several years to implement this plan, I am now convinced that the product and the process can be married. They are meant to function together. In fact, if the product and the process are estranged in the church, the church will not prevail.

The following chapters detail the different components of an effective ministry plan. My hope is that pastors and church leaders will gain insight from this record of and reflection on our ministry pilgrimage. But most important, I pray for two distinct and balanced results: That churches will not only grow numerically but will also produce the quality products

—mature and equipped followers of Christ. Thus they will truly carry out the mandate of our Lord and Savior, Jesus Christ.

After considering this somewhat different approach to "doing church," I pray you will have new hope for the church. In fact, I believe you will become convinced that we must and can change the way church is done in the next generation. If such changes become reality, to God be the glory.

Chapter Four

---oooo---

First Component of
an Effective Ministry Plan:
A GOD-HONORING
PURPOSE

My childhood church did not hold to the authority of God's Word nor promote the true gospel. Years later, as a believer, I found my spiritual pilgrimage in an environment rich in historic, biblical theology. Heritage and spiritual roots were honored. Pop theology was discouraged. My early mentors taught me that I didn't need to invent the details of the faith into which I had been spiritually born. I was quickly introduced to the lesson that I was a new participant in a well-established stream of truth that had overwhelming credentials and time-tested answers. Theological giants such as Augustine, Calvin, Owens, Edwards, and Spurgeon were to be read and revered. The Westminster Confession of Faith was put before me as a guide to direct my understanding of Scripture. I was encouraged to memorize the Scriptures and the catechism of the Westminster Divines, which helped me interpret

God's Word. As a result of this influence, God became a "big God" to me early on, and for this I am forever thankful.

AS A RESULT OF THE FALL, MAN ENTERS LIFE ON A QUEST.

During those first years of spiritual life, I learned the answer to what is perhaps the most important question a person can ask, "What is man's chief end?" The old catechisms answered this question with great insight into God's design for His creation with the response, "To glorify God and to enjoy Him forever." We should be thankful for theologians such as Jonathan Edwards in the past and John Piper and R. C. Sproul in the present, who have brought such attention and clarity to these words. This answer gives credence to the bigness of God and a worthwhile purpose for us.

It is not my intent here to veer into a full theological treatise on God's glory. However, a basic primer on this glorious subject is required because it forms the necessary foundation for a church's ministry plan development. I refer to this primer as "The Story of Glory."

THE STORY OF GLORY

The term *glory* in the Old Testament is the Hebrew word *kabod*. Jonathan Edwards did a wonderful job of explaining this term in unusual detail in his work *A Dissertation Concerning the End for Which God Created the World*.

> The root it comes from, is either the verb (kabod), which [means] to be heavy, or make heavy, or from the adjective (*kaved*), which [means] heavy or weighty. [The term is sometimes] used to signify what is *internal, inherent*, or in the *possession* of the person: and sometimes *emanation, exhibition*, or *communication* of this internal glory: and sometimes for the

knowledge, or *sense* of these, in those to whom the exhibition or communication is made; or an *expression* of this knowledge, sense, or effect. . . . [The Greek word for glory, *doxa*], signifies the *same thing* in the New Testament [as *kabod* does in the Old].[1]

It is this third usage Edwards mentioned, "*the knowledge*, or sense of these, in those to whom the exhibition or communication is made," on which I want to focus. This is, as Edwards explained, "the *manifestation* of [God's] internal glory to [man] . . . and the *communication* of the infinite fullness of God to the creature."[2] It is this revelation of God's glory to man and the effects of God's glory upon man that causes him to know, love, and rejoice in God. In this sense, such heaviness, or wonder, becomes for many, as it were, "splendor," or "renown." God's glory inevitably produces an effect on an attentive person; when the effect is not apparent, the problem lies not with God's glory but in the person. When the apostle John reached his first great conclusion in the early verses of his gospel, he linked together God's incarnation and character with God's glory: "So the Word became human and lived here on earth among us. He was full of unfailing love and faithfulness. And we have seen his glory, the glory of the only Son of the Father" (John 1:14 NLT). When those who knew Jesus best tried to summarize His character and effect on them, they had a favorite word, *glory*.

So, although *glory* describes God, it can also describe the state of man in his original condition at creation. It was God's intention in creation for man to reflect and share His glory. This is part of the meaning of the phrase *made in the image of God* (see Genesis 1:26–27); so the first chapter in "The Story of Glory" tells us that man came into this world with full glory. Thus, at creation, man had all the glory he needed to be fully satisfied. He walked with God.

But the second chapter of "The Story of Glory" tells us that man sinned and fell short of the glory of God (see Romans 3:23). Consequently, being in the likeness of Adam, you and I, and all other persons, are brought into this world stripped of the full glory by which we experience the fullness of satisfaction. We are born fallen.

As a result of the Fall, man enters life on a quest. He is searching for something. He senses the powerful vacuum created by the absence of glory, but he has little idea how to fill that void. He assumes that renown and splendor will come through relationships, fame, success, material possessions, and the like. He goes from garbage heap to garbage heap, from relationship to relationship, from toy to toy, from fix to fix. Yet nothing satisfies. Nothing results in lasting splendor. At best, he gets hints, tastes, and glimpses of glory, but the best relationships, achievements, and possessions fail when they are called on to supply glory. Little does he know that his life, as described by Jeremiah, is like a "broken cistern" (2:13) and must be repaired in order to contain what matters—God's glory.

Now begins the third chapter of "The Story of Glory." God, by His grace, woos the unbeliever into a covenant relationship established through the work of His Son's death on Calvary. Suddenly, as a creature identified with Christ in His death, burial, and resurrection, he receives his initial installment of glory. He is now "in Christ." This is expressed in Pauline exuberance: "to whom God willed to make known what is the riches of the glory of this mystery among the Gentiles, which is Christ in you, the hope of glory" (Colossians 1:27).

But such a glorious position is not without the realities of "a body of sin" (Romans 6:6). A believer's eternal citizenship has been changed (Colossians 1:13), but he or she still remains in enemy territory. A spiritual battle, described by the apostle Paul in Ephesians 6, will continually rage this side of heaven. But now, at least, the believer can experience satisfaction with God and enjoy a growing sense of His glory.

Now begins the fourth chapter of "The Story of Glory." The battles previously described leave the believer torn between living as he is, a new man in Christ, or conforming to the world in which he is temporarily living. He struggles to faithfully find His satisfaction from the glory available in God alone while being bombarded with deceptive promises that he can find renown and splendor in the counterfeits the world can offer. While he was behind the gates of hades, the temptations seemed weaker. Now that he is outside the gates of hades, the question becomes,

"Who will prevail?" Though only Christ can bring him true satisfaction, the lure of the world remains enticing.

So, by the grace of God, trials and sufferings sometimes enter life to erase the illusion that the believer is in control and that his fulfilled dreams can truly satisfy. It is in the shattering of such dreams and hopes that spiritual brokenness takes place. Whether such shattered dreams are voluntary or involuntary, the end result is the same—a believer who now looks to God more and more for his renown and splendor. Such glory added to the believer's life is what Paul describes to the Corinthians, "And as the Spirit of the Lord works within us, we become more and more like him and reflect his glory even more" (2 Corinthians 3:18 NLT).

One of the great secrets to successful Christian living is learning to live life on this earth in view of the full glory yet to be revealed and soon to be experienced in total. Paul exhibited this attitude exactly when he said, "I consider that the sufferings of this present time are not worthy to be compared with the glory that is to be revealed to us" (Romans 8:18).

This process parallels the experience of a mother waiting to deliver her child. The anticipation and agony are bearable and even considered as joy (see James 1:2) in light of the hope of a child soon to be revealed. A Christian must live with the realities of God's glory, yet to be revealed, firmly fixed in his or her mind. Only then do the sufferings of life become both bearable and mildly understandable.

Now we come to the fifth and final chapter of "The Story of Glory." The final episode begins at physical death. Theologians call it *glorification*, because it is at this moment that the believer has his cup filled to the brim with God's glory. He now experiences perfect renown or splendor. After all, he now walks in the heavenly presence of almighty God. Thus ends "The Story of Glory," the only story that truly closes with the heroes living happily ever after!

THE POINT

So, what does "The Story of Glory" have to do with developing a church's ministry plan? It has everything to do with it! Let me introduce the answer to this question by reviewing my own story.

Prior to my personal surrender to follow Christ, I wrongly assumed that to live for God's glory would be everything but an enjoyable relationship. I couldn't imagine a less joyous life. Then, I actually met Christ. Soon, as I grew into my newly birthed love relationship with Him, I was pleasantly surprised to realize that to live for God's glory is to experience the greatest delight a person can know. The very place I suspected held no meaning turned out to be the place that held an inexhaustible supply of glory.

Both "The Story of Glory" and my own personal experience illustrate the point that "life" is about bringing glory to God by sharing His glory. This leads directly to the conclusion that "church" is about proclaiming God's glory so that others may enjoy sharing in His renown and splendor. Thus, when a church is asked, "What is your chief end?" she should be able to give the same answer that is expected of the individual believer, "To glorify God and to enjoy Him forever."

WHAT IS THE CHIEF END OF THE CHURCH?

The first step in designing a plan for the church is to determine her purpose. Purpose is determined by answering the question, "Why do we (as a church) exist?"

Churches often reveal their real answer to this question in practice better than on paper. Or to put it another way, churches often have the correct answer expressed in their carefully preserved documents while at the same time giving an entirely different answer by the way they behave. Their honest answers in practice can vary from "for the purpose of exalting an individual" (usually the senior pastor) to "for the purpose of meeting the needs of individuals" (noble appearing but less than biblical). The only appropriate answer, though perhaps equally well described with different words, is "to glorify God and to enjoy Him forever."

For a church to exist for any other cause in inexcusable. To exist for helping needy people or benefiting a community, as good as these may appear, is unacceptable to God. Why? Because it elevates a good means and twists it by making it the chief end, or because it replaces an all-embracing and demanding purpose with a narrow, lesser purpose.

A LESSON FROM MARRIAGE

This error is even worse than a husband who does the right thing for his wife, but for the wrong reason. Picture a husband bringing his wife flowers. Realizing there is no special occasion to celebrate, the wife asks her husband what motivated such a loving action. His answer, "No reason; just to say, 'I love you.'" As she starts to respond with words of appreciation she is interrupted by her husband. Looking at his watch, he abruptly asks his wife if he can be excused from a commitment he had made to go shopping with her for the day. When she asks, "Why?" his response is, "To allow me to accept an invitation to play golf."

The wife's appreciation immediately turns to fury as she realizes that the flowers are not about "I love you" but rather about "I want to play golf." The very act of giving the flowers becomes repulsive to the wife. So too are the many reasons for a church to exist that are proposed as substitutes for glorifying God and enjoying Him. The church may perhaps be doing the right things yet for the wrong reasons.

MISSING THE MARK

Remember, our Master showed greater disgust for people who did the right things for the wrong reasons (check scribes and Pharisees) than He did for people who simply did the wrong things (tax gatherers and sinners). Like individual Christian moralists, churches that exist for legalistic and benevolent purposes rather than to glorify God and to enjoy Him become the object of almighty God's disgust. And rightly so!

God has scripted the answer to the first question defining the purpose of the church. But the answers pertaining to the questions related to the remaining components of an effective ministry plan are not as easy to come by.

We now turn to a second important component of an effective ministry plan—a faith-oriented commitment.

NOTES

1. Jonathan Edwards, *A Dissertation Concerning the End for Which God Created the World*, section 6; text available at http://www.dallas.net/~trigsted/text/Theend2.htm.
2. Ibid., section 7.

Chapter Five

⎯⎯ ⋙⋘ ⎯⎯

Second Component of
an Effective Ministry Plan:
A FAITH-ORIENTED
COMMITMENT

T he author of Hebrews clearly expressed the importance God
places on His followers living by faith: "Without faith it is
impossible to please Him" (11:6). Let there be no questions about
the importance that "faith living" plays in the life of a church
as well as that of an individual. Ministries that have a mind-set
of seeking to follow the leading of God regardless of the likelihood of success are bound to find themselves living within the
blessing of God.

WILL WE HAVE A FAITH COMMITMENT OR NOT?

When developing a strategic plan for a church, the leadership must first settle this issue: "Will we have a faith commitment or not?" And then it must ask itself, "In what ways will
we demonstrate a faith commitment?" To put it another way, the

church's leadership needs to determine early on which question it is going to ask when facing a decision that carries risk. Will it be, "Is it possible?" or, "Is it the will of God?" I am convinced the latter is the only appropriate question. Or to put the question in yet another way, "To what degree will we risk failure to bring glory to God?"

DOOMED TO FAILURE UNLESS GOD BE IN IT

About the time I reached the midway mark in seminary, I began earnestly seeking what form my ministry would take upon graduation. Several classmates challenged me to explore the possibility of giving my life to the spiritual needs of people in countries without the opportunities of hearing the gospel so readily available here in the States. It was during this time that the president and founder of Haggai Institute, John Haggai, invited me to join Haggai Institute and to work with Third World leaders advancing the gospel. Though intrigued with this ministry, I sensed that such a call was not the leading of God.

SOMETIMES GOD'S WILL
INVOLVES OUR FAILURE.

When I met with Dr. Haggai to inform him of my decision, his response dramatically shaped my life and future ministry. His forceful challenge was to "attempt something so great for God that it is doomed to failure unless God be in it." I couldn't get this challenge out of my mind. It came at the perfect time in my life. Once I adopted this motto, I no longer found myself routinely asking, "Is it possible?" From that point on, the only appropriate question to be considered was, "Is it the will of God?"

IS IT THE WILL OF GOD?

That question has reappeared in some unexpected ways. Early in the life of our church, our handful of first elders was meeting to make some major decisions for our church. One of our elders proposed that we make a bold move and take an unusually large risk (and an expensive one). Upon hearing his recommendation, I responded by saying that though I thought it was a great idea, it didn't appear possible from my perspective. I couldn't have set myself up better for a lesson if I had tried. Now keep in mind I was the one who had been indoctrinating these men with Haggai's challenge, which became our new motto, and stressing the importance of a faith-oriented commitment. I was put in a rightfully humbled position when the same elder responded to me by asking me to quote our often-used motto. No sooner had the words left my lips than he said, "Randy, I would suggest that this recommendation (assuming we have no reason to believe it not to be the will of God) is right on target." We approved the recommendation and found it to be a good decision.

LIMITED GUARANTEE

Many people wrongly assume that seeking to do the will of God with proper motives guarantees success. We need to be aware that it is quite possible to do what we think to be God's will and to do so with the proper motive, and still completely fail. Or to put it bluntly, sometimes God's will involves our failure.

When seeking to make our first church property purchase, we found a piece of property that seemed to have our name written all over it. However, the price of the property was well beyond the reach of the $40,000 land fund we had worked so hard to raise.

Unsolicited by me or anyone else, a group of out-of-town business leaders who knew of our need for property and were friends of our church made us a gracious offer. They were willing to invest in a limited partnership to purchase the property on our behalf. It would be our responsibility to get the limited partnership sanctioned by the Securities and

Exchange Commission and then to make offerings to groups in various cities that these friends of our church would arrange for us to meet. But there was indeed risk.

The earnest required to hold the property while awaiting approval from the SEC was $40,000 (our total land fund). Both business and spiritual counsel unanimously encouraged us to take the risk. We prayed and we waited for government approval to allow us to raise the money. Though the prospectus was eventually approved, the clearance came only a few days before the expiration date of our contract. Without enough time to go to enough cities to make our offering, our time expired and the property was awarded to a backup contract that was submitted after ours. Not only did we lose the property, we lost our earnest money (our entire land fund).

Immediately, monies began to be given to us from some of these same friends as well as unusually generous giving from our people (who would rather have failed attempting something great than never risking failure and accomplishing little or nothing). Within a few months, our bank account was larger than what we originally had. We ended up getting a piece of property that never seemed as ideal as the first piece.

For years, I regularly drove by that original piece of property, which now housed a massive apartment complex. Seeing the size still to be four times the size of our then present property and on a major road with high exposure, I often wondered why God had allowed us to fail in our endeavor. Years passed before He allowed me to get a small glimpse into His "higher ways."

Approximately eight years later, we came to the realization that our original purchased property, even with an additional ten acres purchased, was not sufficient to serve our growing church. In the providence of God, He provided a piece of property two and a half times larger than the piece we had lost and in a much more suitable location. I am convinced we would never have made such a move had we built on the original property.

To further add to this story, not long ago our original site became ground zero of a massive tornado that ripped the apartment complex off its foundation and essentially demolished it. Had we gotten our own way, our church would have been destroyed.

Certainly, when we attempt something we have every reason to believe is honoring to God, and even if we have the right motives, it is still possible to fail. Yet when there is failure, we can know that ultimately we will be better off because of the failure.

RELOCATION

Leading a church with a faith-oriented commitment can be a painful experience. It often reveals the fear produced by the weakness of one's faith. Certainly, I am no exception. The following story illustrates this well.

Earlier, I alluded to our church's undertaking a relocation. At the time, our church was approximately twelve years old. Our leadership unanimously agreed upon this decision. Embracing our well-worn motto, we asked what we thought God's will was regarding the amount of property. Using a formula we felt appropriate to give us that answer, we were astounded to discover that we would need seventy-five acres at a minimum. Though "doomed to failure unless God be in it," we began the preliminary steps toward relocation.

We established a maximum budget we thought generous, but appropriate, and hired two commercial realtors (members of our church) to search for suitable sites. Based on the criteria given them, only one property, a hundred-acre piece, met every specification on the list. However, the asking price of the property was several times more than our allotted budget and the property was already under contract for purchase. The owner dismissed our offer and our real estate agents continued their search.

After making no progress in locating another suitable sight, I asked our two agents to go to the owner and present our offer once again. They returned to say that the owner had no interest in our offer and that the property was still under contract. Yet again, after weeks of a failed attempt to find another appropriate piece of property, I asked these same two men to do me a personal favor and revisit the owner one last time. Though unenthusiastic, they agreed to go. To their amazement, they found that the owner had lost his previous contract and needed to sell the property quickly. He accepted our original offer without negotiation.

Potential Snag

During our period of due diligence before closing on the purchase, I was walking the property. A neighbor who lived adjacent to it, curious as to my presence, asked me who I was. When I told her, she congratulated us for putting the property under contract but quickly told me that we would never get the use permit required to use it for a church. I asked what made her think that. She explained that another neighbor whose property was also adjacent to our property was the president of the largest and most powerful homeowners association in North Atlanta.

She assured me that this lady would fight us and would definitely win. I promptly got her name, gave it to our relocation director, and urged him to become her close friend—and very quickly! Yet, before he could initiate contact, she called him and invited him to attend their upcoming homeowners association meeting. He asked why, and her response was, "To see how enthusiastically I'm going to support your request for a church use permit." He was obviously surprised and curious.

He candidly told her what he had heard regarding her probability of fighting our usage request. She explained that seven years previously she had become a Christian and had been given the gift of faith and a ministry of prayer. She explained that during these seven years, this large tract of land behind her home had been her prayer garden. For seven years she had prayed that God would keep that property for someone who would use it for His glory. She went on to say, "We've opposed one potential purchaser after another and won each time, but when I heard it was Perimeter Church who was buying the property and knew of your reputation in the community, I knew it was God's will for me to enthusiastically support your usage of the property." Our request was subsequently approved unanimously.

Lesson on the Court

Now with such a supernaturally orchestrated event, one would think that we would demonstrate great faith throughout the relocation project. However, this was not the case. Our attempts to raise the money necessary to pay for the property, sell our existing facilities, and raise the money for a new facility all seemed to flounder. The outlook turned bleak. As summer arrived, I left for my annual two-week study leave. I told my wife, Carol, that I sensed God was perhaps leading me to leave Perimeter and search for another ministry. She was shocked, and I found myself grieved over the sense of leading I was feeling. I have never before or since had such a sense. During my last week of study, I stayed in a friend's home in another city. This friend had been a professional tennis teacher for years and had helped teach me to play. Throughout the years I had never beaten him in a match.

AS MUCH AS I FEAR FAILURE,
I HAVE GROWN TO FEAR
THE ABSENCE OF RISK
IN A FAITH COMMITMENT
EVEN MORE.

The day before I was to leave to return to Atlanta, he and I played. I beat him for the first time ever. He was as shocked as I was and immediately challenged me to a match the following morning before I left for home. In his words, "I want to see if this was really a fluke." I didn't want to play, desiring to leave town with a final win under my belt. But I couldn't avoid the match. I believe he beat me "love and love."

Following the match, he commented that though he had seen me play poorly in the past, he had never seen me not try to win. He asked what was wrong. I had to admit to him that I had not tried and that my reason was nothing short of a fear of failure. I knew if I didn't try, I could easily excuse my loss.

God used this episode as a picture to reveal to me that the same was true in regard to our relocation. I wasn't sensing Him leading me to leave Perimeter. I was merely afraid of failure, just as in the tennis match. I had become convinced that we were not going to accomplish the relocation and personal humiliation would be the result.

One morning after I returned home, I was reading Exodus regarding the journey of the Israelites under Moses' leadership. I was prompted to write the following in my journal.

> I've led our church to the seashore. There's no way out, and Pharaoh's army is getting closer and closer. I'm sure the troops are beginning to wonder whether the water is going to part. My confidence in my ability to get the people across the sea has vanished—and that's good—but in light of the diminished confidence I have found myself both frightened and discouraged. Part of my fear is my growing concern that the closer Pharaoh gets, the more unwilling our congregation might be to stand in faith to see the waters part. But I am committed to leading them across those waters— not all will go with us, but win or lose, we're going to finish the race!

As much as I fear failure, I have grown to fear the absence of risk in a faith commitment even more. Now I long to observe the benefits received from being part of a church that demonstrates a faith-oriented commitment to the purpose of glorifying God—such as watching old paradigms of ministry be broken in the formation of new ones, and most important, receiving the blessing of watching God, time and time again, do what some (including me) thought was impossible. Once again, let me illustrate.

BEGINNINGS

After arriving in Atlanta to plant Perimeter Church, we began trying to assemble a core group committed to working with us in raising up this new church. Within a couple of months, God gave us five men and their families to colabor with us in this endeavor. We decided that we needed to secure a place to worship on Sunday mornings. We agreed to set a prayer target, specifically asking God to give us our needed meeting place by a certain date. We all agreed to pray for a secured facility by that date and to participate in locating such a facility.

One person was assigned to look at schools, another to contact real estate agents, another to check out hotels and office areas and similar matters. On the date we had set as a prayer target, we all reported no success in finding an appropriate facility. Early that afternoon, I sat in my home office disappointed that God seemed not to have answered our prayer.

As I sat there, the name of a man, Cecil Day, came to my mind. He was the founder and president of Days Inns of America. Though I had never met him, I had heard wonderful things of his Christian faith wherever I had been in Atlanta. Perhaps only because of a formerly declared faith-oriented commitment, I decided to make a cold call on Mr. Day, not even knowing if he were in town, much less in his office with time to meet with me. As I was leaving, Carol asked where I was going. I told her "to meet with the founder of Days Inn." She was impressed until she found out I didn't have an appointment. When she questioned why I wouldn't call first, my response was that he certainly wouldn't let me see him without an appointment and today was the date for which we had prayed.

Upon arriving at his office, I found his secretary had stepped out of the reception area. Seeing his name on the door behind her desk, I decided to risk it. I opened the door cautiously, only to find Mr. Day leaving his office. I quickly introduced myself to him and explained what I was seeking. I told him I was not asking for a gift but only a facility to rent. He graciously heard me out and sent one of his employees with me to look at the old Day Realty Company headquarters that had just been vacated.

Though it was small and well-worn, it looked like a royal palace to me. I expressed interest in leasing the property and asked what the rental price was. The man told me that Mr. Day was going to give it to us (because it was for a church) at half the asking price. That price came out to $1,700 a month! I nearly fell over in shock. We had no offerings and no savings yet. He then informed me of an additional utility cost of $300 a month. Two thousand dollars a month might as well have been $2 million. Before I could decline the gracious offer, the employee told me that Mr. Day had told him to let him know if I was interested in leasing the space. In his words, "Mr. Day said he may want to give you an additional discount."

I told him we were definitely interested. But it didn't take me long to tally our resources. I was a math major in college, and I could easily figure out 10 percent of $2000—and the difference was meaningless. Yet before I could say anything, the employee had called Mr. Day to tell him of our interest. The man's mouth fell open when he hung up. He looked at me and said, "Mr. Day is giving you quite a discount. He said the price for you will be $50 a month and no utilities." (I tried to get him down to $25! Not really.) Once again, God had honored a faith-oriented commitment.

The benefits of a faith-oriented commitment are many. Whether the advantage of determining the decision-making process, or allowing us to see God do what was seemingly impossible, none, however, compare to the satisfaction experienced from knowing that God was honored and thus pleased.

In 1899, Theodore Roosevelt said, "Far better to dare mighty things, to win glorious triumphs, even though checkered by failure, than to take rank with those poor spirits who neither enjoy much nor suffer much, because they live in the gray twilight that knows not victory nor defeat." Though in full agreement, I would go further. I would say, "Far better to attempt something great for God and fail, and yet still hear Him say in eternity, 'Well done, good and faithful servant; you have pleased Me by your life of faith,' than to succeed in great things yet fail to hear His applause because of our lack of faith."

Success or failure in what is attempted is not the central issue. It is honoring God with a faith-oriented commitment and living out the belief that we live under the control and with the indwelling power of the King of Kings. When a church exists for the single purpose of glorifying God and enjoying Him and operates with a faith-oriented commitment—watch out! There you will find the makings of a prevailing church.

So, early in your strategic ministry planning, embrace a faith-oriented commitment married to a God-honoring purpose, and then get ready to enjoy the blessings of a church that pleases God.

———⬤⬤⬤———

Chapter Six

Third Component of
an Effective Ministry Plan:
A GOD-GIVEN
VISION

I f the purpose of the church answers the question, "Why do we exist?", the vision of a church is determined by answering the question, "What are we seeking to accomplish?" Likewise, if a faith-oriented commitment prepares us to take risks, a God-given vision holds us accountable to take the right risks. The next step in developing a strategic ministry plan involves deciding what God is calling the church to accomplish. Until the church's leadership reaches agreement on this decision, the church cannot move forward.

WHO RECEIVES THE VISION?

This creates an interesting discussion about whose responsibility it is to receive the vision from God. Although the polities of various churches differ from one another and churches may have differing procedures in place to determine that the vision is God-given, it appears that God usually gives vision for ministry to individual leaders, at least as an initial step. In our experience as a church, the clarifying of the vision often comes as members of the leadership team raise concerns or ask probing questions. Although the pastor must accept a significant responsibility for receiving and casting the vision, he should never take this role in an autonomous way. I have found that the elders in our church have had a powerful ministry in my life by schooling my mind. Their combined wisdom has repeatedly helped me see and understand aspects of God's work that I missed because of my limitations. In fact, I have discovered that a significant aspect of God's rule in my heart involves my willingness to hear Him speak through the wisdom of other godly leaders.

I offer the following advice to leadership boards who are seeking to determine what God has for their churches' visions: *Send your pastor on the quest for such a picture. Make taking time to listen to God a priority in your pastor's job description.*

DECISION MAKING

Up until a critical juncture in revisiting our strategic ministry plan, I assumed it best to invite our elders to escort me through any attempt to evaluate our vision. Together we would consider whether God was directing us to a new view of His plans for us or was directing us simply to reaffirm our present vision. Because I normally lead through means of gaining consensus, I asked the elders to work as a team to seek God's leading.

Much time was spent in personal thought and prayer. As time passed, I became more and more convinced of God's leading but continued my monthly dialogue with our elders. Though we ultimately arrived at the same conclusion, I sensed more had been lost than gained in the process. Though we gained consensus, we experienced numerous bumpy roads en route and certainly spent more time debating the issues than seemed wise from the perspective of time stewardship.

After all was said and done, I called church consultant and author Lyle Schaller, whose wisdom I greatly respect, and asked him to evaluate the process we had just completed. His evaluation was profound. He suggested that when we do this in the future I recognize that God would probably initially lead most clearly through me. He described the ideal process as follows.

I, as the pastor, should have, in his words, "gone to the mountain to seek the voice of God." After believing I had heard His voice, I should then go back to our elders, who in our system of polity function as my authority. He recommended that if the elders could not, at that point, affirm my sense of God's leading, then I should go once again to the mountain, spending time listening to God. Whether I sensed that God would lead in the same way I had perceived on my first trip, or whether I sensed that God would lead in a different direction, I should share that with our elders. If, again, they could not embrace this new vision, then perhaps yet another such mountain visit and subsequent reporting should take place. If, however, after three times we could not agree, Lyle suggested that I should then resign. If the elder team and I could not agree on vision, then I, as the subordinate in our polity, should seek another opportunity of service where my vision and my leadership direction could be in harmony.

This approach allows a shared leadership structure to function at its best. It places the responsibility of receiving the vision on one person but maintains the significant role of confirming that vision within a group of fellow leaders. It assigns important initiating authority to a leader without creating an autocratic condition where the vision of the leader cannot be questioned. The approach can also highlight the importance of vision while honoring the biblical principle that although a person's vision may be compelling to him, he cannot assume that the vision can be imposed on others just because he believes it is God-given. Sometimes a difference in vision requires a parting of the ways (note the separation of Paul and Barnabas in Acts 15:36–41).

HOW DOES A VISION COME?

Perhaps the most often asked question regarding vision is, "How do you receive it?" Even as churches differ in their polity, they also differ in their theology. My intention at this point is not to defend my particular theology but rather to share from my personal perspective what I have learned and experienced about receiving a vision.

What Vision Is

First of all, the word *vision* denotes many different things to different people. Some think immediately of a mystical trance or perhaps a particular sign gift. Some would assume an audible voice experience, whereas others would immediately think of a revelation from God perhaps in the likeness of one received by the apostle Paul. My sense of gaining a vision from God is much less dramatic but no less dynamic. Let me describe how I go about seeking a vision from God, illustrated by the manner I went about gaining a vision for the planting of Perimeter Church.

After Dr. Haggai had challenged me to a faith-oriented ministry, I began logging hour after hour alone with God, seated with pencil and paper. Knowing that He alone could reveal to me that to which He would call me, I began each private session asking God to give me ideas as to what that "thing" might be that I could wholeheartedly pursue which would honor Him if it succeeded, but be doomed to failure unless He were in it.

Now I realized that every thought that came to mind had no guarantee of being a thought from God. Yet having cleansed my heart and invited His presence, I was certain that among the many ideas recorded, certain ones might perhaps be prompted by Him—some of which could well be the very thing to which God would call me to give my life.

I am sure I spent nearly a hundred hours alone with God immersed in this communication experience. I kept a clipboard during this particular spiritual discipline and recorded page after page of ideas. I wrote down every thought I perceived as potentially given by God or at least worthy of further consideration. I reviewed them periodically. I asked counsel from those who knew me best regarding many of the ideas but relied mainly on asking God to burn deep within my heart those thoughts that were given by Him. Though I frankly didn't expect to hear a voice, my goal was that certain ideas conceived while alone with God would burn so deeply into my heart and mind that they would be as certain to me as if I had audibly heard from God.

It was during this time that I sensed with great confidence that God was calling me to plant a church unlike any to which I had ever been introduced. The church in my mind's eye would seek such accomplishments that they would be doomed to failure unless God were in it. I was absolutely convinced that if my vision were merely humanly attainable even with great effort, it would not be a God-given vision. The more this vision took hold in my life, the more I realized I would rather fail miserably pursuing it than succeed at a lesser ideal.

I knew that to avoid opposition from traditional thought I would need to be the first person involved, which led me to believe a church plant from scratch would be wise. God used several events to make me believe Atlanta was the community in which to plant the church. As time passed, the clipboard pages continued to accumulate. Several months after beginning the quest, I had a picture in my mind, and described on paper, of a church that I find amazingly similar to the actual church that has evolved over these years.

Adventure in Atlanta

I am always disappointed to hear soon-to-be church planters describe their future church as a "such and such" type of church—referring to a church patterned exactly like a dynamic, well-known church in some other community. The reason for my disappointment in part is that they are forfeiting the possibility of being part of a signature ministry designed uniquely to fit a one-of-a-kind leader and community. But even beyond this, I am jealous for the church planter to experience that sense of profound leading from God that so greatly enhances one's own faith-oriented commitment.

For instance, when we eventually moved to Atlanta, I had just graduated from seminary. Carol's and my first child was less than two months old. The Presbyterian Church in America had hired me to plant a church in Atlanta. They had done so reluctantly. It had been their policy not to begin churches without an established core group, but because I came with my clipboard in hand and the sense of calling so intense to plant from scratch, they were willing to sidestep policy and to approve my request. They had sent us to secure an apartment in Atlanta prior to my graduation and had agreed to pay us $1,200 a month for up to twelve months, as needed. So all was set.

However, I had not considered the fact that my income flow would cease between the time I left graduate school and the end of the first month after arriving on site to begin church planting. We had no plan for our finances during this time, but we did have a sense of calling so strong that we knew (certainly not infallibly) we were to go ahead and move to Atlanta. By the time we actually arrived, all we had left was ten dollars in cash, an apartment without utilities, an empty refrigerator, and an obligation to pay our first month's rent.

Up to the very day we had arrived in Atlanta, we had remained confident that God would supply our every need. But as Friday afternoon ticked away (the designated time for me to pay our rent) all such confidence evaporated. I felt obligated to explain our situation to the apartment manager. Carol and I anxiously wondered what her response would be. As I entered the office, after delaying as long as possible, I said to the manager, "I guess you need our money now?" The manager looked at me with a look of apology and responded by saying, "I am so sorry. I forgot about your payment and have already taken our money to the bank today. I am not allowed to leave money in the office over the weekend." Then the manager continued by asking me, "Would it be OK with you if you paid us first thing Monday morning?"

I looked at the manager with a disguised sense of relief and answered, "Sure, if that helps you, waiting will be fine with me." I hurried home with renewed hope, calculating what we needed God to supply during our unexpected reprieve. Our minimum budget for the remaining weeks until my first paycheck, including apartment rent, was approximately

$600. Now, two extra days renewed my confidence of God's coming provision.

As I entered the apartment, I could see Carol was anxiously awaiting the outcome. I excitedly told her, "Carol, you know God always waits until the last moment to provide His people's needs so as to build their faith. The last moment is not till Monday morning. You watch," I announced to her in somewhat prophetic tones, "God will supply our money through the Saturday mail." I was convinced this was how it would happen for three reasons. One, we had left our new address with many friends who were aware of our excursion to Atlanta. Second, we did not know anyone in Atlanta who could possibly be used to supply our need. And last, I had heard of many Christian leaders receiving exact amounts of financial needs through the mail. I assumed it would happen that way for us as well.

The following morning we found ourselves in the mid-June heat and humidity of Atlanta in an apartment without utilities—awaiting the arrival of the mailman. We anxiously and hopefully kept a lookout until the mailman arrived and passed us by without delivering a single letter. At that very moment my heart sank and my feeble hopes vanished. I began to seriously doubt that God would provide our need. In fact, during that night I was so burdened with the responsibility of a newborn and no means of provision that I awoke, got on my knees, and cried out to God in confusion and unbelief. I knew God was not obligated to provide for us the way in which I felt He would or should. I knew that our move to Atlanta was not revealed in Scripture (the only will of God we can know to be infallible). Yet my sense of having received a vision and call from God was so clear that the events of the moment made no sense. I was honest with God and told Him that I felt abandoned in a mission to honor Him.

The next morning was Sunday. Here we were, in Atlanta as a pastor and family, without a church. We decided to attend perhaps the largest church in Atlanta at that time, First Baptist. We parked and were approaching the front steps of the church when we met an old college friend of mine leaving the earlier service. This friend was one in whose life God, by His grace, had used me while in school. Later, on a couple of occasions, he had sent me a financial gift during my seminary years. Both times I had returned the money, urging him to give it to someone in greater need. Immediately, I remembered that money, knowing he would be more than happy to help us now in our time of financial need. (After all, that was *my* money I had sent back to him!)

WHAT I HOPE IN
DETERMINES IN *WHOM* I HOPE.

After we greeted each other warmly, he asked me what I was doing in Atlanta. I explained we were here to plant a new church. He was intrigued and suggested that we sit on the back pew and catch up during the early part of the service. He said that he would leave before the sermon, having already attended the earlier service. As we were walking into the church, I was already thanking God for His provision. However, before we could be seated, I had a sense that God was speaking to me. Once again, no audible voice, but a sense of conviction in my conscience that was so strong, I might as well have heard an audible voice. I knew God was telling me not to mention our financial need. Not that it would have been wrong for someone else in the same situation or even for me in a similar but different situation. But I knew that God was prompting silence.

Begrudgingly I submitted and remained quiet. Nothing was ever mentioned about financial needs. As the offering plates were being passed, I noticed that my friend was filling out a check. I thought nothing of it, assuming he was preparing his gift perhaps missed in the earlier service. I passed the plate to him. He handed the plate to the usher without adding his check to the offering. He immediately turned to me, stuck the check inside my shirt pocket, and said, "I hope you'll accept this. I've wanted to do something for you for a long time." I immediately said, "I will!" No return of this money! The only question left unanswered, thundering in my mind was, *Did he give us enough money?* It would have been inappropriate to ask how much he had given me, so I just thanked him and anxiously awaited the beginning of the sermon so that my friend would leave and I could check out the amount of the gift.

To my great disappointment, my benefactor did not leave when the sermon began but rather chose to sit through the entire service. That was unquestionably the longest sermon I have ever sat through! I would watch when he turned his head and I would quickly glance into my pocket to see if the amount was in sight—never successfully. Finally, the service ended and my friend left. I quickly pulled out the check to find it to be $600—just what we needed. Some might call that coincidence—but not me! In fact, I'm convinced God intervened in time and space and divinely provided us with that gift. And He did it in a unique and memorable way.

The point is that were it not for a strong sense of a God-given vision, we would probably have never been so eager to launch out with enough faith-oriented commitment to have been sitting there on Sunday morning. We watched God continue to bring to reality that which would have otherwise seemed doomed to failure.

A FRIENDLY WARNING

Before we explore the heart and content of a clearly articulated vision, perhaps it would be beneficial to offer a word of caution to the highly ambitious pastor. Beware of being ambushed by ambition! I am extremely qualified to offer such warning because my life as a pastor has been spent, for the most part, in guerilla warfare with the deceitful internal enemy of selfish ambition. Early on in ministry, I learned that it was easy for me to do the right thing. Yet to do the right thing for the right reason was a different issue. The most dangerous aspect of this warfare is that one can lose the battle yet, because ministry success is defined by visual accomplishment, be heralded as a great victor in the world of ministry.

Whether it is the message we preach or the motive by which we serve, there are always three questions related to ambition that must be addressed. First, is what I am doing or asking other people to do the right thing? Second, is what I am doing or asking others to do being done for the right reason? And third, is what I am doing or asking others to do being done by the right power, the power of the Holy Spirit, not by humanistic self-determination? The object of one's hope in part determines the answer to the second question, which deals with motives.

When one's hope becomes misplaced, wrong motives will certainly follow. I have been reminded, far too often by personal experience, that the object of my hope will dominate my life. If I place my hope in success or man's applause, I will be driven to be successful in man's sight and do what it takes to get that approval. I have learned (am still learning ever so slowly) that improper hope *always* leads to greater sin—not usually, but always. Any hope other than Jesus eventually leads me out on an ever-thinner limb of sin that seems to be all the higher and eventually breaks, dropping me into disaster.

I have also learned that *what* I hope in determines in *whom* I hope. If I want human success in ministry or to glorify my own reputation, I begin placing my hope in ministry promotion, research, and my own abilities. Yet when my hope is in the work of Christ and His abiding power, I will of necessity put my only hope in Christ.

In the summer of 1990, I was away on a July study leave and was keenly aware of the devastation brought about by misplaced hope and selfish ambition. I had received word of several fellow pastors who led large, and what seemed to be significant ministries, who had fallen into grievous sin. I wrote in my journal one early morning the following observation and personal caution:

> Ministries designed to reach the unchurched (thus committed to healthy growth) can easily become vehicles for delivering personal significance through public accomplishment. Large ministries, like large bank accounts, most often become monsters that devour their leaders.

Our goal as church leaders should not be to grow large ministries that reach unchurched people but to build discipling ministries that develop mature followers of Christ who, in turn, reach large numbers of unchurched people.

Though the two approaches to ministry described in my journal may appear to be very similar, the ministry that invests in the individual through discipleship, with the intent of preparing him to reach his lost world, represents an animal much different from the selfish-ambition monster that ultimately devours its leader.

WISDOM

A number of years ago, a small portion of God's wisdom literature began speaking to me quite loudly. The text is found in Proverbs 30:7–9. It reads as follows:

Two things I asked of You,
Do not refuse me before I die:
Keep deception and lies far from me,
Give me neither poverty nor riches;
Feed me with the food that is my portion,
That I may not be full and deny You and say, "Who is the LORD?"
Or that I not be in want and steal,
And profane the name of my God.

Proverbs 30:7–9

I find the author's perception profound. Were I to have only two petitions to make of God and without the insight of this portion of His revelation, I'm sure neither of the author's choices would be mine— and certainly not the part about not giving me riches. Don't get me wrong. A large bank account has never been enticing to me. But riches can be expressed in far more creative ways than simply in terms of money. Would I desire riches in talent, beauty, brains, and opportunity? Emphatically, yes! Would I want my children to have riches in those areas? Once again, yes, without question.

When my first child was born, I was thrilled to have a son. Since I love sports, it was my deep longing that he would be an outstanding athlete. Don't get me wrong. I wasn't being greedy. It made no difference to me whether he made it to the NBA, the NFL, or played major league baseball! When my next child, a daughter, was born, I deep down longed for her to be a beautiful child growing into a gorgeous young woman. Later, however, as both of my sons and both of my daughters began to grow up, I noticed that the kids with abundant riches in athletic ability and beauty were typically the children who struggled the most in demonstrating good attitudes and humble hearts (qualities, for me, having a much greater premium than abilities and good looks).

The wisdom author's request soon became much more my own, for both my life and for the lives of my kids. Now my prayer was, "Lord, don't give my kids poverty in abilities or beauty lest they struggle with their self-esteem; and don't give them abundant riches in abilities or beauty lest they battle with pride. If I can have my request, Lord, let them be contented and competent, somewhere in the middle."

Please don't take this the wrong way. I'm not advocating a commitment to mediocrity. In fact, God's Word clearly teaches, "Whatever you do, do your work heartily, as for the Lord" (Colossians 3:23). I believe this directive includes everything from the way we groom ourselves to the way we show effort in developing our abilities. Certainly, God determines whether we are rich, poor, or somewhere in the middle. It is not sinful to be rich, nor is it a sign of sinfulness to be poor. We must learn to be content "in whatever circumstances" we find ourselves (Philippians 4:11).

The secret is simply this: If I long to be rich in financial wealth, good looks, athletic ability, or ministry success, and I happen to be given such wealth, I am in the most dangerous of positions. However, if I can believe the wisdom of Proverbs 30:7–9 and know the advantages of having neither poverty nor riches, thus not longing for them, the outcome will be different. Then if God chooses to make me rich, more than likely

I will be a good steward of the abundance God has placed in my life. But if I long for riches, and get them, they will probably destroy me.

As a good friend, Fred Smith Jr., once said to me, reflecting on several church leaders who had been ambushed by ambition, "When will the anointing of God be enough?" My prayer for each of us who are naturally ambitious as pastors is that we would see Jesus as our only hope.

REVIEW

A church's vision should include what it is seeking to accomplish *in* the lives of its people and what it is seeking to accomplish *through* the lives of its people. In chapter 1, I referred to this first function under the word picture "a safe home." The "home" work of the church focuses on the lives of its people. I described the second function by using the expression "an effective mission." The "mission" work of the church is channeled through the lives of its people. The next chapter will expand these two functions of a God-given vision.

Chapter Seven

Two Functions of
a God-Given Vision
A SAFE HOME AND AN
EFFECTIVE MISSION

The prevailing church must be a "safe home" and have an outward thrust to the lost and the hurting—an effective "mission." (Later, particularly in chapter 9, we'll be talking about "mission" in the sense of a ministry plan.) It will produce mature and equipped believers and remain contemporary with its culture, responding to and prepared to deal with the realities of today's culture. Its vision will be broad and long enough to encompass whatever time remains in history.

A SAFE HOME

We have already referred to "a safe home" as being one of two central roles of the church. Early in the history of Perimeter, our elders agreed that we would consider our church a safe home when our people were routinely provided with the following:

- *Vital worship* that demonstrates the presence and power of God
- *True fellowship* founded in significant and meaningful relationships
- *Biblical instruction* and *discipleship training* grounded on biblical theology
- *Pastoral care* and *shepherding* directed to the needs of the whole person
- *Equipping and empowering* to do the work of ministry

These criteria served us for many years. They provided helpful guidelines as we evaluated our effectiveness as a church which is a "safe home." Eventually, however, someone pointed out that a significant trait was conspicuously missing from our list. They asked a revealing question: "So, if you are faithful to all the guidelines of a church 'safe home,' what kind of residents do you expect to develop as a result?" The variety of answers we gave only proved one thing—we had a lot of ideas but no clear ideal. We had never clearly identified what the residents of our "safe home" should, in time, ideally look like. We were throwing around terms such as *trained disciples*, *mature believers*, and *equipped Christians*, but had no agreed-upon description for such persons. What kind of Christian was Perimeter designed to produce?

A MATURE AND EQUIPPED CHRISTIAN

I can think of few healthier exercises in our church's life than when we wrestled with this issue and developed a working description. Until this time, it had been easy to hit our vision's bull's-eye—simply shoot the arrow and draw a circle around wherever it hit! We had been focused almost entirely on the process without having a clear target. From this time forward, we agreed the residents we would seek to develop would be called "mature and equipped followers of Christ."

Using that phrase, we have developed a clear outline of measurable expectations regarding the kind of believers we desire to produce. A mature and equipped follower of Christ is one who

- lives consistently under the control of the Holy Spirit, the direction of the Word of God, and the compelling love of Christ
- has discovered, developed, and is using his or her spiritual gifts
- has learned to effectively share his or her faith while demonstrating radical love that amazes the world that it touches
- gives strong evidence of being
  a faithful member of God's church
  an effective manager of life, relationships, and resources
  a willing minister to God's people
  an available messenger to nonkingdom people
- demonstrates a life characterized as
  gospel driven
  worship focused
  morally pure
  evangelistically bold
  discipleship grounded
  family faithful
  socially responsible

Though the wording may differ, the essence of a church's vision should incorporate the development of such mature and equipped believers. Call them by any terms you prefer (*trained disciples, mature believers, equipped Christians*), but such life products should be the fruit of every true church. Why? Because this kind of believer meets Jesus' criteria for discipleship. This kind of believer makes up the core of a prevailing church.

Allow me to include a brief side note here about the mature and equipped follower of Christ. Over the years, I have observed a faulty assumption in the church at large regarding maturity. The majority report among Christians seems to be that Christian maturity is measured by the biblical and theological knowledge a person has assembled coupled with his spiritual commitment. Yet, I am amazed how many people consider themselves mature in Christ but cannot identify anyone who has entered the kingdom because of their life and witness.

Now I know that behavior alone does not declare someone to be mature. Only God knows the motives of a person's heart. But our own Master told us we would determine if a person is one of His followers simply by observing his fruit. Certainly our judgment of such fruit can be faulty and even differ from one observer to the next. Yet fruit is nevertheless an indication of genuine maturity.

Such a description of maturity is not exact, but it does include a crucial emphasis. We tend to think of spiritual maturity as an end—a point of arrival. Without an outlet or a purpose, however, the quest for spiritual maturity can easily degenerate into a kind of Christian narcissism. Do we want to pursue spiritual maturity because that is God's will for us (1 Thessalonians 4:3) or because we think it will feel good to be spiritually mature? In God's plan, spiritual maturity is a means—a life through which the gospel is continually transplanted into new lives.

The guidelines above are primarily designed to help the believer evaluate his own maturity and give the church a reasonable measuring rod to evaluate its work in presenting people "complete [mature] in Christ" (Colossians 1:28).

AN EFFECTIVE MISSION

The other essential function of God's church is that of being an "effective mission." When we decided on a description of "a safe home," our church leadership also decided on a descripton of an "effective mission." We concluded that Perimeter Church would be considered an "effective mission" when we:

- were proclaiming a biblical theology that answers the questions and issues of the culture in which we live
- were influencing all social, political, educational, and professional segments of society with Christians who embrace a biblical world and life view
- were offering to our members the opportunity to be equipped to share their faith

- were facilitating outreach ministries to major people groups in Atlanta based on needs, interests, occupations, age, life experiences, and other factors
- were starting churches of like values throughout the Greater Metropolitan area and ministering to the under-resourced people of inner-city Atlanta
- were sending people and financial resources to support and start ministries in other countries
- were beginning and servicing overseas training centers which equip leadership and establish strong churches in their countries

A CONTEMPORARY CHURCH

The criteria above lead to a significant working conclusion. In order for a church to be an effective mission, its leadership must be intentional about taking every step possible to keep it contemporary to the culture in which it exists. I am certain that many readers will interpret this conclusion as suggesting that the church's style of worship must be trendy or make use of contemporary music. That may or may not be the case. Such decisions depend on the community in which the church is placed or on the specific people group that is being targeted.

The Culture of the 1950s

Allow me to make my point by contrasting the general culture of America in the 1950s with that of its culture at the turn of the millennium, fifty years later. At least three prominent descriptions can be made of American culture in the 1950s.

1. Our culture was accurately described as a Christian culture.

This does not mean that a majority of people in America were Christians but that a majority of Americans held to Christian beliefs and/or values. For instance, if you conducted a random survey asking people's opinion about the appropriateness of allowing prayer in pub-

lic schools, or of having the Ten Commandments in a federal building, virtually everyone asked would have responded that both should
be allowed. If asked their opinion about a mother's right to end her
pregnancy by means of abortion, the overwhelming majority would
have said, "Absolutely not!" If asked whether they believed Jesus was
the Son of God and the Bible the Word of God, again most people
would have concurred.

2. *Our culture was extremely slow-paced.*

Rarely did businessmen and businesswomen travel each week in their
work. Most people lived within a few miles of their place of employment.
Most women worked in their homes and most people stayed at home
most every night. I can remember as a child being at home at night and
suggesting to my parents that we go visit some friends who lived up the
street. We didn't ever call to ask if it were convenient (after all, there
was a good chance that the party line would be busy). We would jump
in the car, drive to their home, and my brother or I would run to the door
and receive the expected and welcomed invitation to come in to visit.

My wife, Carol, tells me that she rarely remembers a night when
her entire family was not at home together (outside their being together
at church or her father attending a monthly officer's meeting of his civic
club). Without question, our culture was slow-paced.

3. *America's culture was considered to be traditional-family oriented.*

Some analysts have tagged households with a working father, a
homemaker wife/mother, and two children under the age of eighteen as
a "traditional family." According to a survey of *Ministry Currents*, this
four-person unit represented 60 percent of all American households in
1960.

The Culture of the New Millennium

Now, let's compare 1950s culture with the culture of the new
millennium.

1. *Today's culture is best described as a secular culture.*

Take the same "man on the street" interview and the responses would be dramatically opposite. Little needs to be said to substantiate this point. The Christian values and beliefs of the '50s are ridiculed and scorned today.

2. *Today's culture is beyond fast-paced.*

Its pace could perhaps be described as supersonic! Carol and I love having people in our home. There's no telling how many guests come through our house annually. Even so, I recently asked her if she could remember a date in recent history where it would be convenient for us to have someone "drop in" on us as my family did on others years ago. Every moment seems to be pre-assigned or committed to multiple activities.

3. *Today's culture is no longer traditional-family oriented.*

Further statistics regarding the family indicate that about half of all marriages end in divorce. The divorce rate among subsequent marriages is even higher at 60 percent. Some two out of every five adults are divorced, separated, or widowed. And more than one-third of all senior citizens are widowed. Among those who will get married this year, more than six out of ten will live together before getting married. Cohabitation has literally mushroomed in the last few years.[1]

Now let's take a look at the church in light of these cultural changes.

The Church of the 1950s

When I was a young student, I was introduced to the gospel at a church across the street from my childhood church. Because most people shared the same general Christian beliefs and values, most church attendees would state with confidence their affirmation of the Apostles' Creed. Everyone learned the Lord's Prayer in grade school and most all could recite the *Gloria Patri*. So, most Protestant churches (the only church I am familiar with) had a similar order of worship, familiar to virtually all of its new attendees.

THE CULTURE OF AMERICA HAS CHANGED AND THE TYPICAL CHURCH HAS NOT.

Due to the slow pace of the culture, American churches had little outside competition for prime time. Because institutional social opportunities were at a minimum and because most people lived so close to their church, it was convenient to be at church twice on Sundays and at least once during the week (typically Wednesday night). With "Blue Laws" in effect, and a high view of the Lord's Day, neither the marketplace, nor sports leagues, nor recreational activities competed with the church or its people's time.

Fifty years ago, the church's menu had only about eight to ten offerings. In addition to Sunday morning worship and Sunday night services, the typical church had children's and adults' Sunday school, Wednesday night prayer meeting, choir, Boy Scouts and Girl Scouts, and Women's Circles. That was all that was necessary in light of the family support and stability found in the traditional family.

The Church of the New Millennium

Today, the dynamic, growing church where I first heard the gospel is still faithful to the same message. Its orthodoxy has never changed—and neither has *anything* else! You can walk into this church today and feel you have stepped back in time—the same worship service, the same basic program offerings, and the same people, just older and grayer. This church today has approximately eighty people on an average Sunday, and the average age of those present is over eighty. I'm sure this story could be echoed thousands of times over throughout the country. What has happened? The culture of America has changed and the typical church has not.

To illustrate what has happened, imagine with me that the most progressive and contemporary church you know was miraculously and entirely transplanted to Mongolia. Assume the people were supernaturally given the language of the Mongolian people, yet the music, programs, dress, and customs of the congregation remained unchanged. What would we expect to find fifty years later? We would probably find a tiny remnant group waiting to die off. We see the same condition in many churches in America today—churches that are out of touch with their culture and totally ineffective as a mission. Even their role as healthy, nurturing spiritual homes has been gradually replaced by a nostalgic repetition of old formulas that no longer affect the daily lives of the few who do attend.

Isn't it ironic that so many of these traditional churches, stuck in the past, would expect foreign missionaries to adapt to the culture of the people to whom they were sent to reach? They would insist upon these missionaries learning the language of these people, wearing the clothing, using the music and styles of their culture as well as the native instruments and architecture. The reality is that the culture of the 1950's America is almost as different from that of the new millennium as is the difference between the culture of America and Mongolia. The problem is readily evident. The tradition-bound church does not really see itself as a mission—only as a home.

How do churches get stuck in time? Several lessons from human experience offer part of the explanation. The church has always struggled to do two things at the same time: maintain faithfulness to timeless truth (God's Word) while at the same time communicating the truth in a timely way and within a continually changing environment. Those challenges can get confused. A church that becomes too attached to a temporary style, as effective as it might at one time be, may end up actually devaluing the eternal truths it is charged to communicate. If the method becomes more important than the message or the audience, that church will not prevail.

Church leaders can profit considerably from studying the book of Acts while asking such questions as, "Why was it so difficult for Gentiles to enter the early church?" "In what ways did Peter, Paul, and others adapt their methods to the variety of situations in which they found themselves while maintaining a consistent gospel message?" "What parallel demands (healthy and unhealthy) do we place on people before we welcome them into the church?"

Methods that have worked in one setting can take on the mantle of universal applicability. A new lyric attached to a very familiar tune or music style may be used by God to transform a community. That effect, however, is not guaranteed if the lyric and tune are transplanted to a place where neither is familiar. Or, to put it another way, we find it very hard to imagine ourselves in a setting several hundred years ago in which "A Mighty Fortress Is Our God" or *The Messiah* were cutting-edge, contemporary music looked at suspiciously by many.

We can't place ourselves four hundred years in the past to listen to a heated discussion about a dangerous and possibly heretical new translation of the Bible into a crude and debased language like English, only to realize the subject under discussion is the King James Version. We must remember that methods and means that may seem to us unchangeable were once the latest thing.

An initial environment of change is attractive to most people. People who are outsiders don't mind change as long as it results in their inclusion. Yet once they become insiders, people tend to resist change, wanting to keep things the way they were when they were attracted. Therefore, the church's leadership often hears its constituency in essence say, "If you change, I will leave." Unfortunately, few people are speaking up for the lost community who are thinking, at least subconsciously, "If you don't change, I won't come."

People tend to think that things will stay the same if nothing is changed. They underestimate the pervasive presence of change in the world. Keeping things externally "the same" hardly prevents change. The changes simply occur in more subtle and devastating ways. So, a church may keep doing what it has always done before, but the effectiveness and meaning of those practices will probably be radically altered. If we want to maintain the same allegiance to the truth, the same effectiveness in communication, and the same faithfulness to our purpose, we must continually change.

G. K. Chesterton once illustrated this point by talking about what happens when you build a white picket fence in your yard. If you want to keep that picket fence the same as when you built it, the worst thing you can do is leave it alone. You must change it constantly—checking, repairing, and repainting it.[2] Faithful church boards understand that if they don't give constant attention to the church facilities, the buildings will eventually fall down. Why are we so reluctant to apply the same principle to the body of Christ that meets in those facilities?

Being contemporary simply means studying one's culture accurately and then asking what can be done, without compromising any convictions or biblical standards, to eliminate barriers to reaching the unchurched community.

THE SCOPE OF A CHURCH'S VISION

Another issue regarding a church's vision needs to be addressed—its scope. Matthew 28:19–20 gives us direction regarding the time scope of the vision. When Jesus instructed His followers to make disciples throughout the world, He punctuated that vision with a time code: "even to the end of the age" (v. 20). The vision of a prevailing church will be broad and long enough to encompass whatever time remains in history. Goals and objectives may have specific time frames and measurable components, but a vision ought to be open-ended. In other words, a biblical vision for the church must be large enough to keep the church busy for a long time!

When Jesus rephrased the great commission in Acts 1:8, He gave us direction regarding the geographical scope of the vision. The church's scope must begin locally and extend to the uttermost parts of the world. Acts 1:8 states clearly, "You shall be My witnesses both in Jerusalem, and in all Judea and Samaria, and even to the remotest part of the earth." This concentric scope provides a picture that includes both the "home" and "mission" aspects of the church's vision. Neither can be excluded without seriously damaging the church.

A VISION GAINS CREDIBILITY WHEN IT CLEARLY RESTATES AND APPLIES BIBLICAL TRUTH.

One way of thinking about these geographical locations is to consider Jerusalem as representing those people who are *both geographically and relationally close* to your church. Judea and Samaria represent those who are *geographically close but relationally distant.* The remotest part of the earth represents those who are *both geographically and relationally distant* from the church. Each of these locations presents specific challenges to the church. The role of witness will vary with each location. This diverse challenge will also require many opportunities for specific equipping at "home" for the purpose of carrying out the "mission" function of witness in those settings. Jesus' words clearly present questions for the church: How well are we doing in accomplishing Jesus' purpose that we be witnesses for Him in each of these various settings? In what specific ways are we impacting our Jerusalem, our Judea and Samaria, and the ends of the earth?

DEVELOPING THE VISION AT PERIMETER

In order to illustrate the formation of a church's finalized vision, allow me to describe the process as it evolved at Perimeter.

The Initial, Conceptual Vision

Earlier I reported spending perhaps a hundred hours alone with God seeking a vision given by Him. When all was said and done, numerous conceptual components became ingredients of that vision. Since we call this entity a "vision," let me describe what I saw in my mind's eye. This was the profile of the church I felt called to plant:

First, I saw a church that could impact an entire metropolitan city by the quality of its disciples. Second, I saw a church geographically broad enough to touch people throughout the entire city. Third, I saw a church sociologically, economically, and culturally diverse enough to reach every kind of people in Atlanta. Last, I saw individual congregations of equipped believers linked together to alter the spiritual, political, educational, and social structures of Atlanta—that is, a church that would bring Atlanta into an encounter with the kingdom of God.

I cautiously concluded that this vision was God-given, but I realized that only time would tell. Without question, the effort would be faith-oriented for two reasons. First, I had no idea how to design such a church, nor had I ever seen or read of a church with a similar vision. Second, and more significant, was the reality that with me as this church's pastor, such a vision was certainly "doomed to failure unless God be in it."

The Final, Written Vision

The point has often been made that a vision is useless until it is written. Perhaps this is a bit of an overstatement. Yet it is typically the case that if you can't write down the vision, then you probably cannot articulate it well enough to cast it for those who are capable of making it a reality. A well-written vision, simple and brief, is a large idea expressed in a way that can be understood, remembered, and repeated to others.

Scripture has an important role in the writing of a church vision. A vision gains credibility when it clearly restates and applies biblical truth. Conversely, a vision that violates biblical principles may be vivid, exciting, and even bold, but it will not be God-given.

Although our overall mission still relates to the threefold breakdown of geographical scope found in Acts 1:8, Perimeter's vision expresses our immediate concern with our neighboring community. Perimeter's written vision answers the question, "What are we trying to accomplish?" in the following way:

We are seeking to bring the people of greater Atlanta and all places where we serve into a life-transforming encounter with the kingdom of God.

Here are the characteristics of such a life-transforming encounter within a community:

- Large numbers of its people become passionately committed to Christ
- Its believers' lifestyles become marked by high moral standards and spiritual integrity
- Its educational, judicial, political, and social structures, etc., begin to be in conformity with the Word of God

Every new member at Perimeter Church is introduced to this vision. We take a significant amount of time to explain the background of each point and allow questions for clarification. Every elder, deacon, and discipleship leader is required to memorize it and embrace it. I can't emphasize enough how important it is that your church's vision be God-given, well articulated in writing, and cast before your people as often and in as many forums as possible. Such a vision is a foundational block in building a prevailing church.

NOTES

1. These statistics have been widely reported. Their implications have been explored in such works as *Complete Marriage and Family Home Reference Guide*, by James Dobson (Wheaton, Ill.: Tyndale, 2000); *Loving Solutions*, by Gary Chapman (Chicago: Northfield, 1998); *Premarital Counseling*, by H. Norman Wright (Chicago: Moody, 1982), and many others. See also "Christians Are More Likely to Experience Divorce Than Are Non-Christians," Barna Research Group, December 21, 1999; and "Born Again Adults Less Likely to Co-Habit, Just as Likely to Divorce," Barna Research Group, August 6, 2001; both articles accessed at the barna.org website; Barna Research Group, Ltd., 5528 Everglades Street, Ventura, CA 93003.
2. Quoted by Joe Garlington in "Finding the Grace Gates," A Leadership Interview, in *Leadership Journal*, Spring 1999.

—∽∾∽—

Chapter Eight

Fourth Component of
an Effective Ministry Plan:
WELL-PRIORITIZED
VALUES

W hat belief, activity, or custom, if forbidden in your church's life, would make its ministry not worth continuing? Or, to put it in different terms, What is most important to your church? Or better yet, What is absolutely indispensable? When you have clearly answered these questions, you have just described your church's values.

STATED AND UNSTATED VALUES

Many, if not most, churches have a set of written values (things desired or expected to be most important) and a set of unstated values (to which the church faithfully adheres every day). Visitors and new members know about the stated values. The unstated values are shared and honored by the insiders. The formal, written values are relatively easy to change. The unstated values seem to be carved in invisible stone. A prevailing church should know and state its values. A church that desires to prevail identifies and honestly evaluates its hidden values because they affect every aspect of church life. And if you think identifying and evaluating those unstated values is difficult, wait until you witness an institution such as a church endeavoring to actually alter its unstated values. But the truth is that unless a church is willing to put its unstated values on the table for examination, any talk about change will be fruitless. More on this later in the chapter.

"WHO WE ARE" AND "WHAT WE DO"

One of our most challenging exercises in developing a ministry plan was to agree on a short list of appropriate values. During an annual officer's retreat (which involved about one hundred elders and deacons), I asked our leaders to gather in groups of ten and make a list of five core values that defined our church. Out of the approximately ten sets of five values, there was amazingly little duplication. Some thought in terms of "who we are" values, such as love or integrity. Others identified "what we do" values, such as outreach or discipleship. Still others listed what I call "how we do ministry" values, such as small groups or cultural relevance.

ONE OF A LEADER'S KEY RESPONSIBILITIES
IS TO KNOW AND TO HOLD HIMSELF
AND OTHERS ACCOUNTABLE
TO THE PRIORITY OF VALUES.

These different perspectives provided plenty of content for a lengthy discussion. We finally arrived at a short list in each of these three categories and developed a description of our beliefs regarding each. Then we asked ourselves an important prioritizing question: "Which of these sets of values are most important to us?" Without question, the list of four values that describes "who we are" as a church won out. Those values included love, integrity, faith, and truth (remembered by the acrostic LIFT). If we don't demonstrate love, hold to integrity, exhibit faith, and embrace the truth, then we should not exist as a church.

The second set of values important to us is our "what we do" values. We have determined that of all the things the church is called to do we will set three priorities as most important to us. These are our "what we do" values:

1. We *glorify* our God through public and private worship.
2. We *grow* in our faith by fellowship and equipping.
3. We *give* ourselves away in service, mercy, evangelism and stewardship.

The last of our three sets of the values are the "how we do ministry" values. For us these include every-member ministry, equipping, cultural relevance, and small groups. Although we educate our leadership about this third set of values, our people at large rarely hear us talk about them. Two sets of values are as much as they can digest and certainly all they can remember.

CHANGING EXISTING VALUES

I mentioned that we would come back to the issue of how to change existing values. The answer to this dilemma is determined in part by what kind of values are targeted for change. Once the formal and the unstated values are out in the open, the real work begins. The most difficult ideals to change are the "who we are" values. The "what we do" and "how we do ministry" values will usually fall in line if the "who we are" values are clearly understood and then preserved.

The character of the church's leadership, in essence, determines such values. One of a leader's key responsibilities is to know and to hold himself and others accountable to the priority of values. Sometimes, the only way to change (or preserve) values involves a change of leadership. An existing or potential leader who cannot subscribe wholeheartedly to the core values of the church forfeits his or her leadership role.

Once the church's "who we are" values have been stated and prioritized, they must be continually guarded and occasionally revisited for clarification. Regular staff evaluations should include a values-oriented component. This will allow the church to reward and encourage those who are demonstrating the desired values and discipline or to remove those who are failing to do so. Hiring or recruiting should also include prescreening for such values in officer and ministry leadership selection. Maintaining high standards of accountability among current leaders also contributes to preserving worthy values and reshaping those that require change.

As for changing "what we do" values and "how we do ministry" values, two suggestions come to mind. First, make sure resources are sufficiently aligned with your church's values. Such resources include prime time, leadership, and finances. For instance, a church's leadership may declare outreach to be a "what we do" value but fail to offer outreach training or outreach events during prime time on the church's calendar. This is certain to undermine the stated values. Selecting influential staff or members to lead the ministries that enhance the values and budgeting for their success are ways to make a value written on paper into a value embraced by the church.

All leadership ministry decisions should be made in strict alignment with the stated values. Many good ministries have been discontinued or rejected at Perimeter merely because they were not in alignment with our "what we do" or "how we do ministry" values. Those decisions were not judgments on the merits of the ministries but expressions of commitment to a clear set of prioritized values. One of the reasons we identify and prioritize values is to aid us in decision making when so many worthwhile opportunities come our way. Without clearly defined priorities to which we maintain faithfulness, our efforts as a church become splintered, chaotic, and ineffective.

In chapter 15 we will address infrastructure. But since we are talking about values in this chapter, let me say now that churches need to design their infrastructure around a multiple-value philosophy. There is always the temptation to allow past ministry successes, a pastor's spiritual gift or talent, or programmatic tradition to elevate a single value to dominate others (especially in the "what we do" values). The American Protestant church has been guilty of this for the last several decades. In my opinion, one "what we do" value has dominated the American Protestant church. That value governs the church's prime time and consumes its best leadership. In our Inquirer's Class for newcomers, I routinely ask those in attendance to guess which in a list of values they think the dominant one has been in Protestant churches in recent decades. I take a hand vote before I tell them my choice. Invariably, my first selection is their last. Let's try it with you. Here is a list of "what we do" values:

- Worship and prayer
- Outreach
- Discipleship
- Education
- Fellowship
- Pastoral care
- Service and mercy

Which of these would you say has been the dominant value? If you picked education, you are one of the rare persons who agrees with me. My conviction begs a question, of course: If education has been the dominating value in Protestant churches, then why are so many church members biblically illiterate? The answer to this question has nothing to do with the *dominance* of education as a value but with the *poor quality* of education.

My argument for suggesting that education has been the dominant value is simple—look at the church's use of prime time and primary leadership. In years past, if you were asked to evaluate the worship service, your response was determined primarily by the quality of the sermon (which typically takes one-half of the allotted time). If you attended Sunday school, your evaluation of it was based on the content of the lesson. If you went to Sunday evening church, your impression would be that most of the hour was devoted to teaching by the senior pastor. If you attended Wednesday night prayer meeting, your experience was probably like mine. Almost the entire evening was spent hearing the same senior pastor do the same thing—teach. The meeting then closed with a few people praying for the sick and shut-ins. With all the prime times filled with teaching and the pastor's weekly schedule filled with preparing messages, it is easy to see why education became the dominant value. Little time or leadership was left for service and mercy, prayer, or discipleship.

With the cultural minimizing of prime time in modern life and with the escalation of fast-paced routines for millions of Americans, we should expect the challenge of designing a multiple-value philosophy of ministry to be increasingly difficult. Get ready for some extremely hard choices. If one were pitted against the other (and in some respects they often are), which would you choose for your church:

- To be huge or holy?
- To worship or to do outreach?
- To have fellowship or education?
- To offer pastoral care or discipleship?

Certainly, choosing the church's values is a challenging yet vital exercise. Later, when we talk about a strategically designed infrastructure we will walk through this exercise. But for now, know that determining the church's values is an absolutely indispensable assignment for the church's leadership. Those values must also be listed according to their priority. Once this is accomplished, it will be time to clarify the church's mission.

———— ⟨⟨⟨∞⟩⟩⟩ ————

Chapter Nine

Fifth Component of
an Effective Ministry Plan:
A WELL-DEFINED
MISSION

Earlier in this book when we have talked about the mission of a church, we have been speaking of its outward reach to the hurting and the lost. But in this chapter we will be speaking of to mission in the sense of a clearly defined ministry plan. In this sense *mission* is best viewed as the *means* of reaching the end—the *vision*. The mission statement answers the question, "How do we plan to accomplish our vision?"

Once again, allow me to illustrate using Perimeter Church's mission (ministry plan). We had to answer the question, "How will we plan to bring the people of greater Atlanta and all places we serve into a life-transforming encounter with the kingdom of God?" We answered this question with four responses:

1. by making mature and equipped followers of Christ;
2. by becoming a church of compassion comprised of

praying people willing to give ourselves away for the cause of the
least and the lost;

3. by building strategic bridges between our church and the communities in which we live, work, and play; and
4. by planting new churches and partnering with existing churches
   across Atlanta and around the word to strategically do the above.

Of these four means to accomplishing our vision, the first stands as one
of the greatest challenge for the modern church. To produce mature followers of Christ requires a radical paradigm change for most churches.

AN INEFFECTIVE PLAN

It is my opinion that the present day church (for the most part) has
embraced an ineffective plan for making mature believers. Though many
embrace the goal of making mature and equipped follows of Christ, most
would summarize their plan for doing so in this way: by providing sound
biblical teaching and beneficial, need-oriented programs. In fact, this
was Perimeter Church's practice for years. Like many of these churches, we also used two seldom-examined questions to measure our success
at being an effective home:

❧ *How many people came to hear the truth?*

❧ *How well was the truth presented?*

These self-examination questions need some attention here. Truthful and helpful evaluation cannot happen if the questions we ask don't
expose the right data. Do these two questions really tell us what we need
to know? The first of these questions does provide a measurable result.
If "exposure to good teaching and a variety of learning opportunities"
summarizes an effective method, then attendance figures indicate success or failure. This standard presupposes that exposure measures effectiveness. But does it actually do so?

One way to test the usefulness of such a question is to apply it to the ministry of Jesus. Was Jesus' effectiveness really determined by the multitudes that showed up for His teaching? Or did He use a different standard (see Matthew 7:24–27)? The crowds who merely heard His words didn't impress Him; He was looking for those who would hear and put His teaching into practice.

The second question, "How well was the truth presented?" invites a subjective evaluation. "How well" seldom means "how faithful to the truth." It usually means "how interesting, how contemporary, and how varied." The term I now use to describe a church with this approach is *program-based*. A church is program-based when its primary method of making mature and equipped followers of Christ centers on the delivery of truth through the vehicles of church programs (for example, seminars, preaching, and classes).

I have already admitted my growing skepticism about the ability of the traditional or contemporary church of today to accomplish the goal of making mature and equipped followers of Christ. For many years my hope lay in the new emphasis on small-group ministry. Our church was one of the pioneers in this movement, only to realize that most small groups eventually settle in to become primarily "care and share" fellowship groups and Bible studies. Though much good came from this emphasis, it still seemed to me to ultimately miss the goal of the church. This is not to say that small groups cannot produce mature and equipped followers of Christ. Rather, it is to admit that most churches, ours included, did not structure our small groups with this end specifically in mind. The means got confused with the ends. We assumed that small groups somehow automatically led to maturity.

We eventually had to admit that small groups simply represented another program in a program-based approach to church. We came to the painful realization that small groups and other merely program-based approaches would not in themselves accomplish either our vision or our mission—not because we didn't have enthusiastic and growing small groups but because our small groups failed to produce mature and equipped followers of Christ.

I came to this conclusion on a summer study leave and discussed my concerns with our elder board. They could have chosen rapid growth over faithfulness. After all, judged by program-based questions, we were doing very well. Instead, the elders urged me to take whatever time necessary to develop a plan that would make our church's lifestyle and structure compatible with the desired product (mature and equipped followers of Christ). Allow me to tell the story of that pilgrimage.

I began my quest with our church staff. I trust this special group of men and women. They are deeply committed to our vision and our values. Early in our discussion one of our staff raised an intriguing question: "Well, who *are* the mature and equipped believers in our church?" As we began creating a list, we saw an interesting pattern developing. Many of the men widely considered mature and equipped were those I had personally discipled. I had the privilege of leading many of them to Christ. Most had, at some point, been part of the small group I was leading. That first discovery led to the next logical question: "What do you do with these guys when you disciple them?" It was the answer to this question that ultimately set our ministry in a new direction.

Until this time, I didn't realize I had been doing anything all that unusual. My approach to discipleship was a combination of ideas and methods that had impacted my own life as a believer. Though my response was not as organized then as it is now, I knew there were basically four ingredients to my approach. Later, we formally added a fifth component, which we recognized as evident.

- First, I made sure the men I worked with were *learning the truth*. In addition to personal teaching sessions, I assigned them tapes to listen to and books and Bible texts to read.
- Second, I spent time *equipping* them—showing them how to use the truths they had learned. I describe this process as "massaging the truth until it becomes understandable and useable." For instance, I learned I couldn't stop once I "taught" them how to personally worship. I had to actually "walk with them" through worship. I needed to show them how to worship and then lead them in worship. Until I did that, I could not consider them well equipped in that area.

- Third, I insisted that our relationship in discipleship include a significant ingredient of *accountability*—asking hard questions and challenging bad behavior.
- Fourth, I emphasized and personalized *mission*—targeting a people group or list of individuals we were in the process of trying to reach with the gospel.
- Fifth, I prayed (*supplication*) regularly for each man in my group and they prayed for each other. We also spent time each week praying together as a group.

As we looked at these components, we saw an acrostic emerge that became a descriptive title for a new approach to ministry that was embraced church-wide at Perimeter. Taking the first letter of each of the five key words, *truth, equipping, accountability, mission,* and *supplication,* we spelled the word TEAMS. We began calling our new paradigm of ministry *TEAMS-based ministry.* With every passing year of ministry I have become more deeply convinced that these five ingredients are indispensable in making mature and equipped followers of Christ.

Not long after this exercise with our staff, I attended a pastors' forum where the business consultant and author Ken Blanchard was speaking. Using a typical business relationship, Ken described the adjustment phases that a person experiences in progressing from a new employee to a veteran and dependable partner. As he introduced his situational leadership concept, I discovered unexpected outside confirmation that we were headed in the right direction. Ken has written about this leadership structure in *Leadership and the One Minute Manager: Increasing Effectiveness Through Situational Leadership* (coauthored by Patricia Zigarmi and Drea Zigarmi).[1] Since you may not be familiar with this concept, let me briefly describe it.

Blanchard begins with the first need of a new learner (whether a new employee or a church member). He or she must be given clear *instructions* and *directives*. But if this learner is typical, he then needs hands-on *coaching* to show him how to use his newly acquired directives. Next, his need progresses to simply requiring *support*. He no longer needs the direct coaching but feels much more secure knowing that a coach is near-by, if necessary. In time, this learner becomes so confident and competent that he can be delegated any duty in his area of expertise. In fact, once he is ready for *delegation*, he is likely to view any attempt to direct, coach, or support him as undesirable and unnecessary. On the other hand, taking a learner straight from accepting basic direction to handling delegation is likely to produce, at best, a disillusioned learner. As I listened to Ken's description of these developmental steps, I couldn't help but realize their application in the church.

In fact, if any institution is guilty of violating situational leadership, it has to be the church. We preach to new Christians about the importance and how-tos of evangelism and then close the message by delegating the task to them. We describe evangelism and then say, "Do it!" Young Christians frequently charge into the world with the best intentions of sharing their faith only to fail miserably. Witnessing seldom turns out the way it was described in the motivating message. These new believers become disillusioned learners, believing that something is uniquely wrong with them. They then vow never to go through that experience again. The next sermon on evangelism becomes little more than a whipping rod, producing guilt.

As I reflected further on Blanchard's comments, the genius behind TEAMS-based ministry became apparent to me. The truth we teach new believers fit Blanchard's definition of *directives*. Effective equipping is the same as *coaching*. Accountability falls into the category of *support*, and mission is the essence of *delegation*. New believers need to be taught the truth and they eventually need to "do it" themselves, but there are significant steps between their starting point and their development into mature and equipped believers.

DIVING IN

Several years ago I decided to surprise my oldest son, Matt, with a high school graduation present he would never expect. I gave him scuba diving lessons and told him we would get certified together. Because of my erratic schedule, I arranged for us to take private lessons to allow more flexibility. After selecting the instructor, I learned that the standard procedure was to spend half of each weekly training session in the classroom and half in an indoor diving pool. Realizing I had an upcoming, lengthy trip to Asia, I asked permission to front-load our classroom time and, in fact, to allow us to do that portion in a self-directed study format. In other words, we would take the materials, study them without lectures, and be tested on our knowledge of diving. The instructor reluctantly agreed but assured us that our test results would have to be exceptional.

For several weeks during my Asia trip I studied diligently. I quickly discovered I knew nothing of scuba diving. I had assumed this sport was simple. You jumped into the water with a hose in your mouth and sucked real hard. Little did I comprehend the risks in this activity. As I began reading my manual, I repeatedly came across such words as *danger, life threatening,* and *serious injury.* For instance, I learned that due to changing pressures at different depths, the diver must ascend slowly and that at approximately thirty feet of depth must "hold" for three to five minutes to reestablish appropriate nitrogen levels in the body. To rush immediately to the surface could be deadly. This warning, however, only gave me slight worry. I still thought the directions were clear, obvious, and simple. Having completed our self-directed study, Matt and I took our exams and passed easily. Now it was time to get wet!

The first week of pool instruction was spent getting acquainted with the diving equipment and practicing distress maneuvers. After learning to clear our masks and use a snorkel and regulator, we were ready to role-play.

Our instructor explained that we would go to the bottom of the twelve-foot pool and operate as "diving buddies"—committed to helping one another in time of difficulty. He described our first test. After we were resting on the pool floor he would randomly point at one of us, indicating the partner in distress. At that time the victim diver was to immediately remove his regulator from his mouth, give the distress signal (arms crossing above the head), and indicate "out of air" (hand motion across the neck). The instructor also spelled out several conditions. (1) We could not abandon the mission. (2) The one in distress could not grab the partner's second stage (the backup regulator). (3) Instead, he was to wait for his partner to place it appropriately in his mouth, allow time to get stabilized, and then slowly proceed to the top. Everything seemed so simple!

Moments later, as Matt and I rested at the bottom of the pool, the instructor pointed to me. In a second, the atmosphere of absolute calm was exchanged for a rush of nervous excitement. Unfortunately, the signal came just as I had ended a long, slow exhale in my regulator. Without thinking, I spit out the regulator while my lungs were completely empty. Realizing my urgent need for air, I gave a very quick distress signal and an out-of-air signal in order to communicate to my son that we needed to speed up the process.

Well, if you knew my son, you would know that he's never been in a hurry in his life—and this time was no exception! He seemed to look casually at me, glance at his backup regulator, and think, *I guess you need some air.* From my breathless perspective, too much time had already elapsed, so I did the unpardonable—I reached out to grab Matt's backup regulator. The instructor immediately and rudely slapped my hand away from Matt's vest. At this point, I decided enough was enough. I pushed up from the pool floor so as to surface and get some much-needed air.

Just as my head was about to break the water surface, the instructor grabbed my legs and pulled me back to the bottom. The role-play had become painful reality! My lungs were now about to explode. Finally, Matt was kind enough to give me his second regulator, and we returned to the surface. After graciously chewing me out, my instructor explained how serious such a move would have been had we been one hundred feet below the surface. I shamefacedly nodded in agreement. But the lecture failed to penetrate my inexperienced confidence. I was still sure that I could quickly master this simple sport.

After several weeks of instruction, the time finally came for our deep-water dives and certification evaluation. Our dive site was several miles off the Florida coast. The first dive took us briefly down to thirty feet. Next we descended to sixty feet. The third of seven dives found us at the maximum depth for amateur diving, one hundred feet. We rehearsed our plan to stay down for the allotted time and then at the instructor's signal to slowly ascend, holding for five minutes at thirty feet before surfacing.

At the end of our "bottom time" on this third dive, our instructor signaled us to begin our ascent. At approximately thirty feet he gave us notice to "hold." Though I fully intended to stop at thirty feet, I suddenly realized I couldn't control my ascent. In my inexperience, I didn't realize I had a pocket of air trapped in my vest. It was rocketing to the surface and taking me with it. Once again, my instructor found himself in that all too familiar position of hanging on to my legs. This time, however, he was unable to pull me down. We were both unwillingly carried upward. As we broke the surface, we both grabbed our heads, suffering an unhealthy lightheadedness. I had done exactly what my instruction manual warned could be life threatening.

Once we were back on the boat we evaluated what had happened. We rehearsed how to avoid the same problem the next time. Then we waited on the ship's deck while we accrued our "surface time," the required period between dives. Meanwhile, I was anxious about the upcoming fourth dive. My self-confidence had been humbled.

As we entered the water the fourth time, I was amazingly conscious of the whereabouts of the instructor. I wanted him right next to me at all times. Dives four and five proceeded without trouble. By our last two dives, we had spearguns in hand, chasing fish, mindless of any fears or concerns. In fact, the dive instructor's proximity gradually became a nuisance to me. It would not have bothered me if he had left us at one hundred feet and gone back to the boat. I was now sufficiently equipped.

This story illustrates well the TEAMS process. My son and I gradually moved from the stage of directives (learning the "truth" about diving), to coaching (offering "equipping" beneath the water), to support (having my instructor by my side offering the "accountability" I needed to provide me security), to delegation (sending me into the deep on a diving "mission" accompanied by confidence based on experience). After this, the instructor was "prayerfully" available from a distance for further training, counsel, and delegation.

Can you imagine after dive number three being told to go down to one hundred feet without the instructor? The problems on that dive had finally gotten my undivided attention. I realized that testing well on the content of the training hadn't been enough. My accumulation of knowledge, though it was the truth, did not negate my desperate need for coaching and accountability from my instructor. Yet this truth is exactly what the church is notorious for ignoring. We give our people directives (truth) and then delegate the task (mission) of living for Christ and serving Him without the necessary equipping and accountability.

It becomes all too obvious that equipping and accountability require life-on-life investment. This is what discipleship is all about. We will look again at the need for discipleship in churches today in chapter 21. Meanwhile, it is worth noting that classrooms, auditoriums, cassette players, TVs, and VCRs create efficient environments for the dispensing of truth but do little for getting people prepared for their God-given missions. Such environments do much for making *knowledgeable* Christians, but do little in the effort to make *mature and equipped* followers of Christ. We gravitate to these environments and methods because they deal with groups, but effective discipleship requires time-consuming personal commitment.

NOTE

1. Kenneth H. Blanchard, Patricia Zigarmi, and Drea Zigarmi, *Leadership and the One Minute Manager: Increasing Effectiveness Through Situational Leadership* (New York: William Morrow, 1985). The above material is based on Situational Leadership® II (SLII®), which is a proprietary learning program of The Ken Blanchard Companies. Its use herein is with permission of The Ken Blanchard Companies.

Chapter Ten

---oooo---

A TEAMS-Based
Church

I was finally able to return to the church leadership with the results of my quest. I told them I had found, with the help of
many people, a biblical approach through which I believed the
church could accomplish its primary purpose, producing mature
and equipped followers of Christ. We introduced the descriptive
term *TEAMS-based church* (as opposed to a program-based
church; see chapter 9). This allowed us to communicate to our
church leaders the difference between where we had been as a
church and the direction in which we needed to move. They
agreed that our church would be considered TEAMS-based
when:

- its primary method of making mature and equipped followers of Christ centers on the use of Truth, Equipping,
  Accountability, Mission, and Supplication; and

- its primary outreach, nurture, education, care, discipline, and equipping take place in small groups where the leader is considered the pastor and the community out of which the participants come (residential, relational, professional, or social) is considered the mission field.

The contrasts between the program-based church and the TEAMS-based church are considerable. The differences on the next page are only a few.

FRONT-LINE TRAINING

During the time of searching for the answer to how to make mature and equipped followers of Christ, an important insight became extremely clear:

Unless the church goes beyond being a safe home for God's people and becomes an effective mission to a lost world, there will not be an environment conducive to making mature followers of Christ.

WE LEARNED THAT TO EFFECTIVELY
MAKE MATURE FOLLOWERS OF CHRIST,
THE CHURCH MUST BE INTENTIONALLY
"SCATTERED" THROUGHOUT
ITS COMMUNITY.

I define discipleship as "having a life product, being intentional about imparting that product, and spending enough time doing the right things to impart that product." Discipleship must take place on the front lines of mission. People often say they meet weekly to be discipled by someone at a restaurant. I immediately respond by asking if this is where they think their discipleship begins and ends.

Program-Based Church	TEAMS-Based Church
1. Its ministries are mostly *centralized*.	1. Its ministries are mostly *decentralized*.
2. Its effectiveness is evaluated by the quantity and quality of its *ministries*.	2. Its effectiveness is evaluated by the quantity and quality of its *disciples*.
3. Its people ask the question: "What is the *church* doing?"	3. Its people ask the question: "What are *we as believers* doing?"
4. It views the *professional staff* as the pastors.	4. It views the *small group leaders* as the pastors.
5. Its members are expected to be *consumers*.	5. Its members are expected to be *ministers*.
6. Its small groups function as "homes" that meet the needs of God's people.	6. Its small groups function both as "homes" that meet the needs of God's people, and as "missions" that reach the unchurched communities.
7. Its strategy for making mature believers is *singularly focused* on the delivery of truth.	7. Its strategy for making mature believers is *multifocused* on the requirements of truth, equipping, accountability, mission, and supplication.
8. It places *undue emphasis* on the importance of *teachers*.	8. It places *equal emphasis* on the importance of teachers, pastors, and disciplers.
9. Its *classroom ministry* is more important than its small-group ministry.	9. Its *small-group ministry* is more important than its classroom ministry.
10. Its staff and elders focus primarily on *deciding* and *directing*.	10. Its staff and elders focus primarily on *discipling, pastoring,* and *teaching*.

Discipleship may include a discussion across a restaurant table, but it certainly doesn't end there. Jesus said to those He discipled, "Follow Me." Then He led them into the intensity of battle for God's kingdom, right to the front lines. He watched them fail and coached their efforts. It was there that the disciples began asking the right questions. It was there that the disciples gained perspective in applying the truth that they had been learning on an ongoing basis. Yes, Jesus and His disciples broke bread together at the table, but their shared meals were only a small part of His effort to grow them into mature and equipped followers.

"SCATTERED"

Another insight that emerged during this process had to do with the means of taking the discipling process to the front lines of battle. We learned that to effectively make mature followers of Christ, the church must be intentionally "scattered" throughout its community. We easily think of the church as "gathered" corporately for weekly worship, but we don't have a clear picture of what it means to be a church "scattered." That lack is a clue to the absence of a "mission" commitment to complement the "home" commitment of the church. If we can't see the church scattered, effective scattering is probably not occurring.

Believers who clearly understand and accept their mission when they walk out of church are the same believers who find their greatest joy and anticipation in gathering for worship again. Why? Because their mission mind-set gives them many opportunities to see God work, and they are eager to meet again with others who share their commitment. Scattering and gathering complement each other in the life of the church. Without intentional and mission-oriented scattering, the gathering simply becomes a weekly worship and teaching session.

The "world's largest church, Yoido Full Gospel Church in Seoul, South Korea, has been a source of curiosity and amazement because of its size. Its growth has been exponential for years. Why? Because they have taken seriously the task of "scattering" as well as "gathering." But more important, they have kept the task of mission as important as the task of home (even in the church scattered). We see this approach mirrored time and time again, particularly in Asian, Latin American, and South American cultures.

Many American pastors have observed what happens in these other countries and have tried to import the same approach to the U.S. They have experienced a high rate of failure. As our staff studied these effective Third World churches, we wondered why such an approach appears to be nontransferable into our culture.

The answer, we believe, lies in the substantial differences between our cultures. Here are a few of those many differences.

1. Americans have been spoiled by high standards of excellence.

The people of our churches can turn on their radios and TVs at any time and find the likes of Chuck Swindoll teaching brilliantly. Meeting in a home to be taught by a moderately gifted layman pales in comparison. The same is true of music. Yet in many of these foreign cultures *any* teaching and *any* music is highly appreciated and embraced.

2. The simpler and slower lifestyles of these cultures compared to the prosperity and mobility of America allow for little travel away from home.

Leaders and attendees alike have few conflicts with active participation in their home groups. We, in America, might miss two out of four weeks due to travel schedules. We live with overbooked calendars.

3. These cultures typically provide very few competitive, alternative amusements and distractions.

In America we have our social clubs, our neighborhood athletic programs, and our fast-paced society. A house church is just one more choice of activities. Our relational cups can be filled in many different venues. In many foreign cultures, the only social activity of life is found through the church—more like the first half of the twentieth century in America.

4. People in these cultures more readily submit to God-given authorities.

This includes ecclesiastical authority. In talking to a lay pastor of this type of scattered church in Guatemala, I discovered that their house church pastors would not go out of town for their first year of service—not even for vacation. After a year, if an apprentice had been raised up to assist, the lay pastor could ask permission to be absent. Only if allowed would he miss his home church responsibilities.

When I challenged this idea as perhaps a little too heavy-handed, my Guatemalan friend looked at me with a puzzled look. He said, "You are shocked at the respect and obedience demonstrated to our God-given church leaders who keep watch over our souls; we are shocked at the indiscriminate submission you show to your marketplace bosses. They tell you Monday morning to be in Chicago on Tuesday and you immediately comply, even if you have to miss your kid's championship soccer game on Tuesday afternoon." His point was well made.

Carl George tells the story of talking to the pastor of Yoido Full Gospel Church, Paul (David) Yonggi Cho. He asked Pastor Cho what the secret was to his church growing by 20 percent each year even after reaching several hundred thousand in size. His answer was quick: "That's simple. You divide your church into groups of ten and require each group to win at least two people to Christ each year."

Carl responded by saying, "Yes, I understand, but what happens when those groups don't win two people a year?"

Cho answered, "But they do!"

In dismay Carl said, "But what *if* a group doesn't win two?"

Pastor Cho immediately responded, "We would discipline them. Jesus said, 'Follow Me and I will make you fishers of men.' If ten people do not win two people over the course of a year it means they are not following Christ and need to be disciplined."

Pastor Cho's words indicate the chasm between Third World cultures and ours. We struggle in America to faithfully discipline for sins such as adultery. We are certainly far from disciplining believers for their failure to effectively evangelize!

The point of these illustrations is not to say we should discipline Christians who fail to share their faith or require our small group pastors to forfeit vacations or require pastors to get permission from their supervisors when they need to travel. Rather, it is to say that we must recognize the differences in our cultures and humbly seek to identify principles that are transferable. Ministry approaches used in other cultures must be translated before we can expect them to work in ours. Having said that, let me add that we can learn much from our brothers and sisters overseas.

"SCATTERED" PRINCIPLES

In my personal research six principles have emerged that stand out regarding the success of the church functioning well when scattered. They are as follows:

1. Leaders must have no other major responsibilities in the church. To be a pastor or a discipler is a time-consuming ministry for a layman.
2. The groups must meet at different times for the different functions of "home" and "mission" in order to keep both clear.
3. Prayer and fasting must undergird the decentralized ministry.
4. Good ministries (often conflicting with the *best* ministries) have to be scaled back.
5. Leaders must be equipped weekly and over long periods of time.
6. There must be an extensive apprentice-training program.

Our efforts to translate these principles into our own culture, schedules, and appetite turned out to be a challenging process. But we were committed to living out a well-defined mission. More will be discussed later, but let me say now, we knew when we began that several changes had to take place. Prayer and fasting had to take on a greater emphasis in our ministry. Leadership roles had to change. Elders had to move from functioning primarily as directors and decision makers to focusing on pastoring and discipling. We had to redesign the roles of our staff, moving many of them from program oversight to people oversight. This meant describing and hiring new staff positions. We had to call a moratorium on starting new ministries that were competing for resources with such a decentralized ministry. And very important, we had to significantly enhance our leadership training. (More about this when we discuss strategy.)

"GATHERED" AND "SCATTERED"

When all was said and done, our mission to make mature and equipped followers of Christ could only become reality by becoming a TEAMS-based church. Frankly, we didn't fully understand the implications for such a dramatic transformation. When I came back to the elders to share my new insights, I gave them a broad background by putting the types of changes needed in the context of the historical church (though certainly overly simplistic, I think the following historical overview makes the point). I illustrated the church in five distinct paradigms that have appeared over the course of church history. Each paradigm applied one or more of the location and purpose terms we have been using. The location terms are *Gathered* (G) and *Scattered* (S). The purpose terms are *Home* (H) and *Mission* (M). I entitled the original paradigm the "New Testament Church." It is described in the following box.

Gathered		Scattered	
H	M	H	M

The New Testament church functioned as both gathered (as a large community fellowship) and scattered (from house to house). Throughout the New Testament the church functioned both as a home (meeting the needs of its people) and as a mission (reaching out to win the lost). The dynamic of the early church as recorded by Luke in the Acts of the Apostles is unquestionable. Though maturity might have been suspect in much of the early church, its zeal and effectiveness was considerable.

Next we move to the "Dark Ages Church."

Gathered		

This box is basically empty. Much has changed since the New Testament Church. Though the church was still gathered, it was no longer functioning in a scattered capacity. Because the church had abandoned the truth (for the most part) we have erased the H. Thus, God's people were not cared for or nurtured. Certainly the church had no evangelistic zeal; thus, the removal of the M.

Next we come to the "Reformation Church." Great advances were accomplished in the Reformation. The most important was that the Word of God was brought back to the people of God. The church, though still meeting only as gathered, now brought the function of home back to the church. God's people could now be taught and fed the truth. However, the Reformation movement was not known for its mission to a lost world as much as a ministry to the existing church (I realize some will disagree with me on this, but allow me to make the greater point). Thus, our descriptive box looks as follows:

Gathered		
H		

Note how many churches, even today, that embrace the Reformed faith are modeled in this manner. They are most often traditionally gathered only and are satisfied with the task of proclaiming the truth even if there is no evangelistic fruit (even when amidst a productive harvest). Although I fully and proudly embrace the Reformed faith, I am also grieved at the failure in mission so many of our churches experience.

We now move several centuries through time to come to the modern-day church. In the 1970s, a new paradigm in the church began to emerge that would redefine the way church is done. It began with Willow Creek

Community Church in Chicago and is typically described as the seeker-sensitive church. This church is illustrated as follows:

Gathered			
H	M		

At last, mission was brought back to the church. Willow Creek proved that mission is not the task of only parachurch organizations. It can be done well by the Bride herself. Seekers could be invited into the gathered church and hear the gospel effectively presented there.

Though Willow Creek has in recent years pioneered small-group (scattered) ministry, it has been known more as a church that gathers to do its mission. We call it a "front door church." Even at Willow Creek, I think it is fair to say that most small groups do not scatter for the sake of mission, but primarily for the function of home, though this has been changing more in recent years.

Then along came a new model championed by church growth consultant Carl George. It is typically referred to as the Meta-Church—the changing church model. This was Carl's attempt to see the church scattered—his application of lessons in exponential growth learned from the overseas church. This church is depicted as follows:

Gathered		Scattered	
H	M	H	

I know it was Carl's greatest intention to see the church's "scattered" function as both a home and as a mission. I have discussed this at length with him. I know he would disagree with me, but my investigation of the churches used as models of the church as a mission in its decentralization do not prove to be so (from my vantage point). Even as God has used Bill Hybels through Willow Creek, He has also mightily used Carl George to shape the church more into the likeness of God's intentions.

From my perspective, there is one more shift that needs to be made. Adding the M to the church scattered is one of the greatest challenges the church faces today. Whether or not this is called a TEAMS-based church is irrelevant; the important thing is that this change gets implemented. When this happens we will actually be functioning in much the same paradigm as the New Testament Church.

Gathered		Scattered	
H	M	H	M

Little did we realize, when we began the journey of trying to answer the question of how to make mature followers of Christ, that we were, in essence, suggesting a radical change in the way church is done. We appreciate the valuable lessons learned from others and are eager to stay faithful to the vision God has given us. The best way we can do that is to make sure that our mission statement clearly outlines a means to achieve our vision.

AFTERTHOUGHT

As I noted early in this chapter, I admit to a narrow focus in the historical overview I presented. I wanted to illustrate the general course the church has followed from age to age. God has certainly preserved and extended His church throughout history. Ultimately, the very existence of the church today is first and foremost a tribute to the One who said, "On this rock I will build my church, and the gates of Hades will not overcome it" (Matthew 16:18 NIV).

I am also convinced that in every era, there has been a core within the church that has, in one way or another, preserved the New Testament model of the church. For example, I might mention the Methodist awakening of the eighteenth century, when Anglican clergy such as Whitefield and the Wesleys brought mission, discipleship, and the scattering aspects back to the church. John Wesley, in particular, was painstakingly methodical in his pursuit of discipleship. The principles that we call TEAMS can be clearly seen in what Wesley called his "class meetings." In these highly structured small groups, biblical truth, equipping for ministry, accountability, mission, and supplication were the order of the day.

The main point of the overview was to clearly focus on the next challenge: What must the church today do in order to live as a New Testament church in our time and place? That challenge must guide us every step of the way.

———∞∞∞———

Chapter Eleven

Implementing a Well-Defined Mission

Both the vision and the mission of the church require expansive boundaries. Each of them expresses part of such a large effort that it is bound to fail unless God be in it. So, the well-defined mission includes not only how God wants us to affect our immediate surroundings and our most distant targets. God has called us to take our witness beyond our local residence. Jesus told His disciples that their witness should extend beyond Jerusalem and Judea. That was familiar, friendly territory. He specifically named Samaria so there would be no confusion about His intentions. Samaria represented people who were geographically near but relationally distant. Jesus told His disciples to go to the first people they thought about as well as the last people they cared about.

THE CITYWIDE MISSION

Today, America's cities represent Samaria for many Christians. For those already in cities, certain neighborhoods or areas of the city clearly replace Samaria in Jesus' geographical commission. God intends for His gospel to be shared liberally even with those with whom we have very little in common but who are close enough geographically to be recipients of our loving servanthood and our gospel message.

The church's leadership (led by the pastors) needs to spend much time listening to God for both a vision and a mission related to the metropolitan center and the rural communities around them.

To illustrate the development of such a citywide mission, allow me once again to use the story of Perimeter Church. Remember that a mission facilitates a vision. The mission we arrived at goes beyond simply "making mature and equipped followers of Christ." It also includes the following three statements:

- by becoming a church of compassion comprised of praying people willing to give ourselves away for the cause of the least and the lost
- by building strategic bridges between our church and the communities in which we live, work, and play
- by planting new churches and partnering with existing churches across Atlanta and around the word to strategically do the above

As I mentioned earlier, from the time John Haggai challenged me to a faith-oriented commitment, I spent many hours seeking to receive a vision from the Lord. When I emerged months later with a clipboard filled with the description of a future church, I was deeply convinced it was "doomed to failure unless God be in it." The reason, in part, was because I felt called to start a church with the intention of literally impacting an entire metropolitan city. The city's geographical breadth and social, economic, ethnic, and cultural diversity seemed to squelch any hope that one church could make such an impact. But the longer I spent dreaming and praying, the more hopeful I became that this vision could be fulfilled. In spite of the obvious obstacles, I believed that God just might move in this way after all!

Perimeter West

It became obvious that a church making such an impact would have to be decentralized into all geographical areas of the city and would have to include many cultures. The expression "One church—many congregations" seemed to express the concept. Within two years of beginning Perimeter Church, we felt it was time to birth a second congregation that we called "Perimeter West." I preached an early service at our original location, left before the service had ended, drove approximately ten miles to our new congregation, and walked in just in time to preach. Then, before that service was complete, I got back into my car and drove back to our original congregation, once again, just in time to preach in the second service.

Perimeter In-Town

I did this for almost three years until we hired an assistant pastor to do most of the preaching and to run the day-to-day ministries for Perimeter West. By this time, we had built our first permanent facility, located about ten miles north of our original meeting location. When we moved in, we split the congregation. Those who lived north went to the new facility. Those who lived south began meeting in a rented facility about five miles south of our original location. Once again, I preached at two locations each Sunday morning—an early and late service at our new facility and a middle service at our new southernmost location, which we called "Perimeter In-town."

This process continued for a couple more years until the right assistant pastor was hired. Now there were three congregations under the Perimeter umbrella. Very soon after this, we birthed a new congregation from those attending the service at our newly built facilities. Now there was one church and four congregations. We had a single elder and deacon board and we had one combined staff for all four congregations. We all financially contributed to a combined budget, but otherwise each congregation (after becoming financially sound) was responsible to cover its own needs. I preached at the original congregation three weeks a month, and on each fourth Sunday of the month would rotate to a different congregation. As complicated as it sounds, it all worked surprisingly well.

Changing the Model to Be True to the Vision

About two years after beginning our fourth congregation, the elders asked me why there was not a fifth congregation on the drawing board. Our original vision had been for approximately one hundred congregations to be planted in my lifetime (assuming God were to keep me at Perimeter throughout my ministry). In order to answer them honestly, I drew upon my family as an analogy.

A VISION IS SACRED
IF GIVEN OF GOD AND
NOT TO BE DISCARDED BECAUSE
OF ANY PERSONAL PREFERENCES.

At this time we had four congregations. Ironically, I pointed out, Carol and I now had four children, each born the same years as each of the four congregations. (No, that is not where this is headed!) I explained that I was very happy with four children but would not be disappointed to have Carol announce a fifth on the way (which would not have been our choice). However, at some point in time, perhaps at the announcement of child number seven or eight, I would be hard-pressed to get excited. Likewise, I was now senior pastor of four growing congregations. In my mind, we had reached some kind of stopping point.

This, however, was not good enough for our elders, and neither was it good enough for me. We all knew something had to change—either our vision or our model. The dilemma was clear. On the one hand, our pastors, staff, and elders were all very pleased with our present arrangement and strongly resisted a change. On the other hand, a vision is sacred if given of God and not to be discarded because of any personal preferences.

We gathered the entire staff at a local retreat center. Our goal for the day was to design a plan to solve our dilemma. How could we continue to add congregations without in some way changing the other aspects of our system? By the end of a long day we had made progress in identifying and understanding the problem, but unfortunately we had made no progress in solving it. To say the least, I was discouraged.

I returned late that afternoon to my office, sat back in my desk chair, looked up at the ceiling, and called out to God. I admitted I had no answers and needed help. My secretary had stayed late and was in the next office. About the time I had finished placing my frustration and inadequacy before God, my secretary informed me that I had a call from Carl George. She asked if I wanted to be interrupted. My answer was an emphatic "Yes!" God had just "interrupted" my prayer with an answer.

Though I had briefly met Carl George on one or two occasions, I was surprised that he remembered me. After exchanging greetings, Carl told me that he had just landed in Atlanta for a speaking engagement. He told me that during his flight the Lord seemed to be putting my name on his mind. He continued, "I feel a bit strange calling under these circumstances, but do you have any idea why God might want me to call you?"

Of course I did! Here was one of the most noted church ministry architects and consultants calling me! And calling immediately after I had told God we needed help. The timing was divinely delightful. I quickly told Carl our situation, and we agreed to get together. That conversation eventually led to our hiring him to consult with us.

The most important thing Carl did for us was to verify our own suspicions. In order to keep true to our vision we would have to change our working model. In his opinion, our model was reasonably efficient, and he thought we could expand to about six congregations using this system. However, it was also his strong belief that if we were determined to keep our vision (which we remained convinced would require at least one hundred congregations to accomplish), we would have to change the model.

We hired Carl to design a plan to recommend to us. He supplied us with many perceptive observations and a suggested plan of action. Although we realized his final recommendation had great merit, we were not convinced it fit who we were as a church. In our opinion, it was a design that centered too heavily on the senior pastor and the parent church. During this period of consultation and exploration, however, God significantly used Carl to get us to the next step.

PERIMETER MINISTRIES INTERNATIONAL

Believing there had to be another model that would keep us faithful to our vision and honor our mission, we commissioned four of our best thinkers (an elder from each of our four congregations) to meet with me and creatively explore new options. After many months of meeting, praying, and deliberating, we created a new vehicle to safeguard our vision. We named it Perimeter Ministries International (PMI).

Our plan was to create PMI as a servant organization of the four congregations. As a parachurch organization, it would have its own board of directors and would have no direct authority over any of the congregations. Within a year, each of the four congregations of Perimeter Church would particularize (become organized churches) and the assistant pastor at each congregation would become the senior pastor. To eliminate confusion, each church would also rename itself. This plan included a new name for the original Perimeter congregation, but the staff and elders of the three other congregations insisted otherwise.

The function of PMI would be to accomplish the three tasks the "one church–many congregations" had been doing as a combined ministry:

1. To plant and serve new churches
2. To direct combined resources from the multiple congregations to enable effective ministry to the under-resourced and urban areas of Atlanta
3. To broker ministries and materials throughout our congregations so as to enhance the effectiveness of each church

More important, with a common vision and solid relationships, we could work together to accomplish what no single church could do alone.

We immediately hired a director of PMI, a director of church planting, and a director of urban ministries. The only issue left unresolved had to do with my role. This was one of those occasions in which I was deeply grateful to be surrounded by godly men who were committed to the vision and mission of the church. As I listened to the elders discuss my fate, I realized that I was not indispensable in God's plan. Others owned this ministry as deeply as I did. Their deliberations had little to do with my wishes and likes and a lot to do with their commitment to see that God's very best be done. Some of our elders felt I should move full-time with PMI. Others felt I should stay at the original congregation in an effort to continue leveraging our oldest and largest church. The latter approach was based on our intent to continue modeling from a grassroots level what we wanted to see happen in our multiple churches.

It was my heartfelt conviction that I should stay in the saddle of a local congregation. My passion was still to be close to the heartbeat of a prevailing church. We ultimately decided that I would be full-time pastor at Perimeter and serve as chairman of the board of PMI.

After ten years of being one church—many congregations, we were now four churches. Under this new structure, we immediately began a new church and then another. We quickly found our new arrangement made it much easier to start churches reaching different people groups. The new church plants had less direct impact on the staff and schedules of the existing churches. As I write, we now are starting numerous new works each year and expect that to increase annually. Our pastors enjoy a monthly forum, as do many other leaders from the different congregations (such as youth leaders, administrators, and children's pastors).

I see the day coming soon when our multiple churches (along with partnering churches across the city) can choose needs to target within our city and quickly bring its resources to bear upon them. For instance, each church could encourage some of its members to run for virtually every school board comprising the Atlanta school systems. Then PMI would equip each elected member to understand education from a biblical world-and-life perspective. Similarly, government, media, and medical leaders and institutions could be targeted with resources from these many congregations capable of bringing Atlanta into a life-changing encounter with the kingdom of God.

The PMI vehicle has carried our vision well for over ten years. But vehicles must constantly be re-evaluated and even replaced as the ministries they carry grow and change. Even now as I write, we are once again contemplating a newer model or vehicle to carry us the next ten years or so. Though visions remain the same, the vehicles that carry them must often be replaced with newer models.

I long to see the day that our citywide dream becomes a reality. Although I'm realistic and know that the realization of this dream is not a future certainty, I do believe that the vision is achievable and, by God's grace, may well become a reality. The existence of such a thought-through mission accomplishes two important goals. First, it helps keep a God-honoring vision alive. Second, it holds before our leaders a well-defined ultimate objective.

THE GLOBAL MISSION

Many years ago, while I was seeking to discern God's direction regarding my future ministry, I read a book that considerably shaped my thinking. Dr. Haggai loaned it to me with his endorsement that it was one of the most influential books he had ever read. It was the autobiography of John R. Mott. (Unfortunately, it is out of print today.)

True to Dr. Haggai's prediction, it made a distinct impact on my life. John Mott is best known for his instrumental role in the formation of the Y.M.C.A. But more important, he was used by God to send thousands of college-aged young people overseas in mission endeavors at a time when few even considered such ventures. John Mott coined the slogan, revived later by Campus Crusade for Christ, "The Great Commission in this generation." Through what later became known as the Student Volunteer Movement, untold numbers of lives were changed. One of the memorable statements from Mott's book that has stayed with me is this: "He who multiplies the doers is worth more than he who does the work."

Though I now realize that God has different roles and gifts within His body and all are equally valuable, Mott's comment freed me to realize that staying within the States was not a less noble call. From the time God began to direct me to plant a church in Atlanta, however, I committed to Him that I wouldn't consider the work successful unless we were truly effective in multiplying the doers of ministry.

For this reason, the importance of including a global component in the vision and mission of the church is indispensable. The global aspect of our mission is captured in the fourth and final statement of mission:

- by planting new churches and partnering with existing churches across Atlanta and around the world to strategically do the above.

The days of Americans being the primary leaders in foreign lands are, for the most part, over. Our people may still be needed overseas but now primarily in support roles and behind-the-scenes positions. Of course this is not the case among certain unreached people groups, but those are the exceptions. The tide has shifted. Our previous comments about vibrant Third World churches indicate that we have plenty to learn from our brothers and sisters overseas. The giving and receiving has become increasingly reciprocal. We need their help as much as they need ours.

Each church must discover what its greatest contribution to the world can be. The challenge is for a church to make that determination and then give itself wholeheartedly to it. The fields are ready for harvest. The opportunities are varied and amazing. It is always difficult for our global ministry leadership to turn down supporting many wonderful causes that are not in alignment with our vision and mission. But we have been assigned to certain "fields," so we have to stay clearly and somewhat narrowly focused. Church planting is *our* best contribution, and to this end we operate somewhat myopically. This certainly has lead to some misunderstanding among outstanding Christian mission organizations with whom we choose not to cooperate. We never seek to devalue their specific calling. We simply want to be true to the specific calling God has placed on our church.

DEFENDING THE MISSION

Let me conclude this chapter by saying a word or two about the importance of defending the mission. This has to be one of the most important duties of the pastor, church staff, and elders. Responsible and faithful leaders will make certain that the good does not rob church ministries of the best.

When we decided to make the shift to become a TEAMS-based church, we identified our greatest threat to a successful transition—we named it *the monster*. This term refers to the many good and excellent ministries that already existed or would be lobbied into existence. We recognized that they might appeal to our vision and values but would not fit our mission. Such good ministries, if welcomed, would eventually devour the resources necessary to accomplish the mission and vision.

After looking realistically at the damage that could be caused by eliminating existing ministries (many greatly appreciated), we finally decided that the best we could do was to "cage" those ministries, as opposed to "killing" them. Now the staff scrutinizes every new ministry idea based on how well it is aligned to our mission. Our elders do the same in approving our annual budget, holding us accountable to stay aligned to our mission.

Notice that I said, "aligned to our *mission*," not "aligned to our *vision*." It is amazing how easy it is to take any good ministry and make it fit into the vision. But the mission is a different story. The process shares many similarities with arguments for a balanced budget. Everyone is for a balanced national budget, but when the discussion begins on how we plan to do it, the sparks begin to fly. Trust me, sticking to the mission and keeping ministries aligned with it causes a great deal of discomfort.

Two specific ministries stand out that illustrate such a struggle. The first involves a ministry that has existed since the beginning of our church—adult Sunday school. The second—Boy Scouts—was a ministry being lobbied for by several influential leaders in our church. If you want to find ministries to cage or to kill with little emotional trauma, these are not the ones to pick.

I emphasize that hard decisions will repeatedly have to be made if you are going to defend your mission. If you are an elder in your church, let me say again that one of your highest calls is to defend the mission as well as the values and vision of your church—even if it means the elimination of your favorite ministry. If you don't defend the mission, then who will?

We tell our newcomers when they are investigating Perimeter Church that it is not our goal to make them happy. It is our goal to get them blessed. For this to be a long-term reality, you and I, as leaders of the church, must not ask the question, "Is it a good ministry?" If so, we're probably going to end up asking, "Why not do it?" The question you and I must ask is, "Is it the best?" If it's not, then our final question will be much different. We will then ask, "Why do it at all?"

In our survey of an effective ministry plan we have now addressed the God-honoring purpose, the faith-oriented commitment, the God-given vision, well-prioritized values, and the well-defined mission. We are now ready to start talking about job descriptions.

---∾∾∾---

Chapter Twelve

Sixth Component of
an Effective Ministry Plan:
BIBLICALLY BASED
JOB DESCRIPTIONS

Question several employees of any successful company regarding who their customer is or who their employer is and you will get both consistent and accurate answers. Ask a group of faithful members of most churches who the customer of their church is, or who serves the roles of employee and employer in the church, and you may well get a different response from every person. Can you imagine a company operating smoothly with this kind of confusion? No wonder so many churches today are ineffective! Clear and well-communicated job descriptions are as important for a church as for a business.

In the earlier chapters I raised questions, which when answered leave the leadership of a church with a clear understanding of that particular component of their ministry plan. The question to be answered regarding job descriptions is, "Who will be responsible for what in accomplishing the vision?"

Perhaps the first and most critical issue for a church to settle is to clearly identify the church's leadership and determine how that leadership will function. Though this may sound elementary, it remains an unsettled and disputed issue in many churches.

Robert H. Schuller correctly defined leadership and its importance when he said:

> Leadership is the key to church growth. If the church is really to succeed in its mission of witnessing to the non-churched world in the Twenty-First Century, it must develop aggressive, dynamic and inspiring leaders.
>
> . . . Leadership is thinking ahead, planning for the future, exhausting all possibilities, envisioning problems and dreaming up solutions to them, and then communicating the possibilities and the problem-solving ideas to the decision makers. *This* is leadership.
>
> In any institution, the leader is the [person] who is thinking ahead of everyone else. He is not living in the past but in the future, for leadership draws its inspiration from future projections and not from past accomplishments. The leader is alert to movements, trends and evolving developments. He is literally thinking longer thoughts than anyone else is—and expressing them effectively![1]

WHO IS THE LEADER?

Who should carry out the leadership functions in a church? Is it the pastor, a team of staff leaders, an elder board, or a board of directors? Several other key questions cannot be avoided:

❧ *Does leadership responsibility equate to authority?*

❧ *If designated leaders do not have authority, then who does?*

❧ *How do different leadership roles relate to each other in the area of authority?*

These are complicated questions. Wrong answers or confusing ones create chaos in churches. In fact, pastors, staff, and lay leaders of churches in virtually every community struggle with these issues.

So let's try to bring some order to the confusion. Our primary guide will be the Scriptures. I hope to help churches be able to better define the job descriptions of the various necessary leadership roles within their congregations. In this chapter and the next we will address the job descriptions of elders, deacons, pastors, staff, and the laity.

I realize that churches differ in their polity as well as their terminology for church leadership. I am using the term *elder* to refer to what the Bible calls the *episkopos* in the Greek language. This is the office for which the qualifications are described by Paul in 1 Timothy 3:1–7 and Titus 1:5–9. Other English translations often used include the terms *overseer* or *bishop* for this role. I am using the word *deacon*, which transliterates the Greek term *diakonos*, to describe a special servant-leadership role whose qualifications are described in 1 Timothy 3:8–13.

Because the emphasis in this chapter is on biblically based job descriptions, I encourage leaders in churches that do not use biblical terminology in their local church job descriptions to rethink their reasoning carefully. A church structure that includes only two categories (pastor and lay person) leaves out too much clear biblical teaching. A church structure that strictly assigns all the biblical terms (elder, deacon, bishop, pastor, evangelist) to professional staff runs the danger of disenfranchising much of the body of Christ. The biblical guidelines for job descriptions include some flexibility, but one of the underlying principles should be the following: *A healthy local church structure will include roles that express each of the biblical leadership positions. These two are elders and deacons.*

DEACONS: SERVICE

We begin with a brief word about deacons. The specific responsibilities of deacons are not laid out in a prescriptive manner in Scripture. In other words, the deacons' serving role appears to be quite broad. However, the role is generally described in the historic record (Acts

6:1–6), when this office was instituted. On that specific occasion, deacons were appointed to serve food daily to widows. That original involvement of deacons, however, does not determine the specific job description for deacons today. The central insight given into the role of the deacon is found in verses 2–4 of the passage. Deacons do that which frees the elders to do their job.

Thus, it appears that the job description of the deacon is to be shaped by the needs of the elders. We assume that, as illustrated in the early church, the focus of deacons will be directed to those with special needs within the church. Just as needs vary from community to community, time to time, and church to church, so we expect that the specifics of the deacons' job description will remain flexible.

Over and over I observe churches whose leadership is plagued with emotional conflict between an elder board and a deacon board. Clearly, both groups are biblically validated, but their working relationship within Scripture requires more attention. Deacons feel somewhat insignificant in relation to elders. Confusion frequently exists, for example, over who has responsibility for the budget and finances of the church. Does money management fit the "holy" stereotype of the elder board or the "practical" stereotype of the deacon board? Many describe the role of deacon as minor-league duty before being called up to the major leagues, where the elders function.

The truth is that the position of deacon is not one of spiritual authority but one of service. Deacons are appointed or called to specific and temporary duties. Deacons serve elders and serve on behalf of elders. Elders, who hold the "keys" to God's kingdom (see below), do carry authority, yet they are charged to exercise it with a servant's heart. Deacons serve in a place of high honor. The first martyr in the Christian church was a deacon. The descriptions of Stephen's courage, faith, and witness in chapters 6 and 7 of Acts refute any nonsense thinking about the role of deacon being minor league.

Regarding who has final responsibility over the budget and finances, go back to our earlier discussion on values. Who sets the values of the church? I suggest that this is the responsibility of the elders, who comprise the spiritual authority of the church. Now, if the highest spiritual authority in the local church does not also have final authority over finances, a contest of power invariably follows. Imagine what would happen in a church where the elders defined the value of outreach but the deacons determined the budget. Suppose the deacons allotted no money in the budget for outreach. Let me ask you, which group in reality has established the values? Obviously, the deacons.

This does not mean that deacons have no say in establishing values or budget. A wise elder board seeks input from many sources. The issue is that the Scriptures entrust the final exercise of authority in the church not to an individual (such as a senior pastor) or any group that grasps power, but to a specific group representing the congregation called to wisely and prayerfully direct the church.

My continuous counsel to the leadership of new church plants is to never allow the deacons to assume such responsibility. Let their role regarding finances be to distribute the monies to the needy as allotted by the elders of the church. I find that deacons who are truly called of God to their roles are excited to get out of administrative responsibilities in order to devote themselves to hands-on ministry to those in need. I would advise that as the church grows and the staff becomes capable of doing so, they be allowed to be involved in the spadework of budget preparation, leaving the responsibility of final approval to the elders.

ELDERS: GIVEN THE KEYS
OF THE KINGDOM OF HEAVEN

Let us now address the job description and role of the elder. Such a job description can never be clear without a biblical understanding of the authority vested in this office. To gain such an understanding, we once again turn to the passage discussed in chapter 1, Matthew 16:13–19. However, this time we are gong to focus on what we can learn about the role of the elder.

After asking the Twelve about the public's opinions concerning Him, Jesus asked His disciples who they thought He was. Peter, speaking for the apostolic band, replied, "You are the Christ, the Son of the living God" (Matthew 16:16 NIV). To this confession Jesus responded, "You are Peter, and upon this rock I will build My church" (v. 18 NASB). Our Lord then made a declaration with far-reaching implications: "I will give you the keys of the kingdom of heaven; and whatever you shall bind on earth shall be bound in heaven, and whatever you loose on earth shall be loosed in heaven" (v. 19 NASB 1977).

What Are These Keys?

What are these "keys of the kingdom of heaven"? What are these "binding" and "loosing" functions of the keys? Keys have only two functions: to lock and to unlock. Possession of the keys represents authority to open and to shut. Since the new Israel of God, the church, is no longer a theocracy governed directly and immediately by God, God has determined that the church will function under His delegated authority—human leadership. Thus the "keys of the kingdom" represent the authority Christ has granted men to govern His church.

The church's leadership is granted specific authority "to bind" (to derive from God's Word and to enforce that which is obligatory) and "to loose" (to determine and allow that which the Word says is permissible). Spiritual authority thus discerns what is required and what is permitted. Why is this so important? Because the teaching of the Bible is often principle-focused rather than case-specific. Thus, wise judgments as to the application of scriptural principles to particular situations must be made. The "keys of the kingdom" are emblematic of the authority given to the church to determine the proper standards of biblical faith and practice and to carry out biblical discipline when required.

Who Holds the Keys?

So, we must answer the logical question: Specifically to whom in the church is this "binding and loosing" authority granted? Church history offers three predominant replies to this query.

As we noted earlier, during its foundational years the Roman Catholic Church adopted the view that the keys were given uniquely to Peter. According to this understanding, Peter alone received the keys and thus became the first pope, passing along the keys to generation after generation of popes throughout history.

But this interpretation appears to be based upon faulty exegesis. In the Greek language of the New Testament, the name Peter is *Petros*, meaning "small stone or pebble." But a different word, *petra*, meaning "a large boulder or underlying bedrock," is used in reference to the "rock" upon which Christ promised to build His church. Jesus thus employed a play on words in His reply to Peter, saying in effect, "Simon, you are Petros, a small pebble, solid but transitory. But it is upon the immovable bedrock of your confession that I am the Christ, the Son of the living God, that I will build My church." It was not Peter himself, but rather his confession of faith in Jesus that formed and maintains the foundation of the church.

Moreover, although the English *you* in "I will give *you* the keys," "whatever *you* bind," and "whatever *you* loose" is in its singular form in the Greek text of Matthew 16:13–19, the exact same teaching of Jesus in Matthew 18:18 uses the plural. The same truth is also conveyed in John 20:23 using the plural. In light of these other passages, it seems apparent that in Matthew 16, Jesus was speaking to Peter as representing the other apostles standing with him. Jesus indicated in His teaching that the proper recipients of the keys are several in number rather than being a single, particular person.

This observation leads to the second and third historic understandings of this passage. Both of these understandings rightly recognize the plurality of the key-holders. The distinction between the views lies in their differing identification of the key-holders.

The first of these last two views is represented by the practice of some modern churches that suggests that Jesus has given the keys of the kingdom to each individual believer. According to this view, when a believer exercises saving faith in Christ he is using the keys to let himself into the kingdom. Churches adhering to this belief generally devalue the importance of church membership and may reject it altogether. If people believe they are Christians, they are automatically members of Christ's earthly church. Those holding this view often teach that membership in a local church is superfluous.

One difficulty with this position is that it makes each believer an authority unto himself and negates the need for church leadership and discipline. Advice, admonition, and rebuke offered by other, more mature believers have no more authority than any other opinion. This view also raises problems by its impracticality. What Christian who has fallen into habitual sin would use his set of keys to remove himself from church fellowship?

THE PHRASE *CHURCH DISCIPLINE* HAS BECOME A SHOCKING OXYMORON

The last and most plausible of these views of the key-holders' identities has been adopted by the vast majority of Protestant churches throughout history. When He gave the keys of the kingdom, Jesus spoke not only to Peter but also to all the assembled apostles. He gave them collectively the authority to "bind and to loose," that is, to speak and to act for God. Jesus did not make them infallible (note Peter's repeated failures and denial). Nor did He make them sinless or perfect (note Judas' presence). This corporate apostolic authority was subsequently transferred through the laying on of hands to biblically qualified and selected elders in local churches (1 Timothy 3:1–7; 4:14; Titus 1:5–9). *The church has always been healthiest when she has lived under the leadership of wise elders functioning as a unit under the guidance of Scripture.*

Such God-ordained elders continue to hold the keys of God's kingdom in the church today. It is their responsibility to protect the purity of the church and the honor of God's Word through biblical discipline of Christ's flock. They open church membership to professing believers, withhold membership from non-Christians, build up and encourage the repentant sinner, and dismiss the unrepentant from fellowship.

Again, as was true with the original disciples, the possession of the authority of the keys does not guarantee some sort of infallibility on the part of elders. Their decisions must be based on biblical grounds, and they do have boundaries. For instance, elders do not ultimately determine whether a particular person is or is not a Christian. Only God knows that with certainty. Nevertheless, the decisions and declarations of the elders carry the authority of God in such a way as to determine whether or not a person is to be treated as a Christian. It is in this context of understanding that the full meaning of passages such as Matthew 18:15–18 and Hebrews 13:17 is revealed:

"If your brother sins, go and reprove him in private; if he listens to you, you have won your brother. But if he does not listen to you, take one or two more with you, so that 'by the mouth of two or three witnesses every fact may be confirmed.' And if he refuses to listen to them, tell it to the church; and if he refuses to listen even to the church, let him be to you as a Gentile and a tax-gatherer. Truly I [Jesus] say to you, whatever you shall bind on earth shall be bound in heaven; and whatever you loose on earth shall be loosed in heaven." (Matthew 18:15–18 NASB 1977)

Obey your leaders and submit to them, for they keep watch over your souls as those who will give an account. Let them do this with joy and not with grief, for this would be unprofitable for you. (Hebrews 13:17)

In the passage from Matthew, "Let him be to you as a Gentile and a tax-gatherer" means, "Let him be treated as a nonbeliever," which in practice means removing a person from church membership. "Leaders" in Hebrews 13 refers to those ordained as elders in the church, who plainly have the authority and the responsibility to faithfully direct God's church.

The Will and the Wisdom of God

In these Scripture passages and others, the Lord has indicated the nature of the authority He wishes to be exercised in His church. Other passages speak of the authority God intends to be exercised in the other two of the three foundational institutions He has ordained for the benefit of society: the state and the family (see Roman 13:1–7; Ephesians 5:22–6:4). A specific leadership authority has been granted the right and the responsibility to bless the good and discipline the wicked in each of three areas:

- Parents in the family
- Civil magistrates and governors in the state
- Elders in the church

For the most part, members of society obey the laws of the state, if for no other reason than to avoid the civil and criminal penalties of law breaking. The authority of parents appears to have been in decline over the years, as the practice of loving but firm corrective discipline has been widely abandoned. The authority of the church was disregarded long ago, in part because of faulty interpretations of the passages cited above and in part because of the unwillingness of the church to enforce biblical discipline even when such a responsibility is recognized and badly needed.

Unfortunately, clear biblical teaching on this subject is almost extinct today. It is so foreign, in fact, that you may still be scratching your head. The phrase *church discipline* has become a shocking oxymoron. For this reason, perhaps I should address an important issue to further enable you to understand the authority given to elders. There is a distinction, I believe, between what I call the authority to determine the *will* of God and the authority to determine the *wisdom* of God. The point is that unless they contradict the infallible Word of God, elders' decisions regarding moral and ecclesiastical matters always declare the *will* of God even though they often fail to declare the *wisdom* of God. Allow me to illustrate.

We have already pointed out that *parents* have been given authority from God over their children (Ephesians 6:1). Likewise, the *civil magistrate* (government) has been given authority over its citizens and residents (Romans 13:1–2). With this in mind, how would you answer the following question? If a child chooses not to obey her parents, even though their orders do not contradict God's Word, has she violated the will of God? Of course she has. She may argue, "Show me in the Bible where it says to be home at ten o'clock at night and I'll do it, because I certainly want to obey God. I don't think it's God's will for you to arbitrarily set my curfew time."

If this were your child, your response would more than likely be, "What I say is God's will for you because I am your parent." But what if you gave in to her desires and told her to be home at two o'clock in the morning? If she came in at ten till two, would she be "in the will of God"? I say yes. In this case, you, as the parent, have declared for your daughter what is the *will* of God. In my opinion, however, you have failed to declare the *wisdom* of God. Establishing a curfew is your *authority* responsibility; establishing a right and healthy curfew is your godly *wisdom* responsibility.

For an interesting study on the contrast between the will of God and the wisdom of God exercised in a home, read the account of Nabal, Abigail, and David in 1 Samuel 25:2–38. Nabal's authority in his home was honored *(God's will)* even though Nabal exercised that authority stupidly *(not God's wisdom)*.

The same holds true for God's other institutions, the civil magistrate and the church. When our church decided several years ago to relocate, I often heard the question, "Are we sure this is the will of God?" I was glad to know that such was the heart and concern of our people. At a meeting to update the people concerning the progress of the effort, I addressed this matter. My comments went something like this:

> In response to the often-asked question, "Is this relocation the will of God?" I have some very important news. Without any question whatsoever, God has made it known with perfect clarity that it is His will for us to attempt the relocation.

I could sense the thoughts of our people as I said this. *Man, this doesn't sound like Randy. In what ivory tower has he been meeting with God?* So I concluded by saying:

> I can say so with such absolute confidence because our elders voted to do so. They have prayerfully exercised their authority responsibility. Now, although I know it's God's will to pursue the relocation, I have no such certainty that the decision reflects the wisdom of God. Only time will tell.

We apply this principle in other settings. When two members of our church have a financial dispute in a business matter and follow Paul's instructions to the church at Corinth to take the issue to the church rather than the courts, we see the value of this teaching. After argument is made from both sides, the elders have to make a decision. Whatever that decision is, the party ruled against must see that "whatever you [the elders] shall bind on earth shall be bound in heaven" (Matthew 16:19 NASB 1977). Thus, the decision made on earth (assuming it doesn't contradict the Word of God) becomes that upon which the Lord places His approval. This is to carry the authority of His will. In many of the same decisions, I'm sure eternity will reveal much lack of wisdom, even some mistakes. Nevertheless, even as in a civil court of law, the authority rests in those holding the responsibility to make the decision.

Similarly, the real test of a child's obedience and honor toward his or her parents doesn't involve obeying just the wise and thoughtful rules but also the fickle and unwise ones. In Luke 2, Jesus was content remaining "in My Father's house" (v. 49) while Mary and Joseph searched for him frantically. But when they insisted He return to Nazareth with them, He went willingly. That's the point at which Luke declares, "And Jesus grew in wisdom and stature, and in favor with God and men" (v. 52 NIV). The test of submission to authority doesn't come when that authority tells us we can do what we want but when that authority blocks our will or reaches a conclusion we are sure is wrong.

I have belabored this point regarding the authority vested in elders for two reasons: (1) to emphasize the importance of wise submission by those under authority, and (2) to impress upon us the sober responsibility God has given to those who hold this office. Their declarations express God's will. That role should never be taken lightly or proudly. Elders must humbly insure that their primary responsibility never gets lost behind lesser duties, such as directing programs and attending monthly meetings.

Key Tasks of Leadership

Those who are elders have been called to "shepherd the flock of God" (1 Peter 5:2). They are described as those who "watch over your souls as those who will give an account" (Hebrews 13:17). Since such responsibilities are made so clear in Scripture, allow me to suggest that those who hold the keys to the kingdom must give themselves primarily to pastoring, leading, teaching, and discipling. Such roles can be performed in a variety of different manners, but should never be allowed to degenerate to merely administrative functions.

Staff Versus Elders

Of all the organizational dilemmas that have challenged Perimeter Church, perhaps the most significant has been trying to determine how to maintain the line of distinction between the responsibilities and authority of the staff and those of the elders.

When our church was only a couple of years old, one of our elders spoke with great emotion during one of our meetings regarding a concern he had. A church member had asked him a question regarding a program in our church about which he was unaware. He said passionately that something was wrong when an elder was so uninformed. At this point, another elder, who was seasoned and grayed enough to really look the part, challenged all of us elders to rethink our role in decision making. He suggested that regarding decision making, the elders should deal only with policy and leave the programming decisions to me in my specific duties as pastor, to our staff, and to the many ministry team lay leaders. Seizing on the fact that most of the elders were businessmen, he asked how many of the companies for which they worked operated with the board of directors making the day-to-day operational decisions. We decided then that the staff would be responsible for programming and the elders would take care of policy making, discipline and theological issues, staff personnel issues, and approval of our overall mission plan.

But how easily all this was forgotten. Within a few years, our elder ministry team was composed of totally different people. Standards of operation had not yet been written. We weren't very consistent in our elder orientation, and those who had joined us from different church backgrounds held different assumptions. I had fallen into the mistaken habit of bringing major program decisions to the elder team. Most of these issues were ones the staff had already debated for hours. When the elders tried to debate the same issues in the half hour allotted for discussion, faulty decisions resulted.

On one occasion, seeing where the discussion was headed, I observed that our staff had already been down that road only to find a dead end. With that, one of the elders spoke up in frustration and said, "If you want us just to rubber-stamp the staff's decisions, then we don't need to be here. Either you guys make these decisions or allow us to labor long enough on these issues to draw our own conclusions."

I called Lyle Schaller for some outside counsel. I told him of my frustration and asked him to what degree elders should be involved in making program decisions. His response was that the only lay elders who should be participating in approving or disapproving programs were those who volunteered on the average of fifty hours a week. I think he was perhaps intentionally overstating the case to make his point. But his rationale was that it takes full-time involvement in the overall life of the church to understand the implications of one program on the whole of the ministry. Only broad experience allows a leader to see how approval of one ministry may well take the resources away from another.

Though the elders no longer spend time making decisions about programs, I do go to them from time to time for counsel about programming issues that may impact our vision or mission. I value their wise perspective on major decisions. Our elders are pleased that they can give their time primarily to matters such as pastoring me, holding me accountable in my spiritual pilgrimage, laying hands on me and praying over me for lengthy periods of time each month, and dealing with the policy and personnel issues of our church. We now take more care and time with the orientation and training of new elders. Many of the principles we have developed for discipleship have specific application in the preparation of elders for their unique leadership ministry.

Size of an Elder Board

The question regarding the size of an elder team or board must be addressed. There are no numerical biblical directives to be heeded. Because I believe that an elder's job is permanent until he surrenders his ordination for some reason or needs to be dismissed, and because we can never have too many pastors, teachers, and disciplers, we elect and ordain as many who are qualified and willing to serve. From this pool of elders, three are appointed each year to join a team of six other elders to serve for three years, giving leadership to the church by serving on what we call the Elder Ministry Team (EMT). We have nine ruling elders on our EMT.

We have nine ruling elders. Although those elders and I have an equal vote on any issue, in reality ten elders is probably too many for this highly specialized role. Lyle Schaller argues for boards of either five or seven. We have chosen a larger size due to travel schedules and periodic transfers. Also, our elder team divides into two task forces each month to prepare for our monthly elders' meeting. That makes each committee just the right size. So ten seems to work well for us. By the way, we also find it helpful to include in each yearly class two elders who are relatively new to our church so that we don't find ourselves always thinking in the past. At the same time, we like one of three elders per year to have previously served to make sure we maintain continuity with our past.

The choice of these three men each year is as critical as the election of new elders each year. Let me suggest that you require your leadership not only to meet the character standards described in Timothy and Titus but also to study your ministry plan adequately and commit full support to it. These leaders form the backbone of the congregation, and they provide the supporting supervision for the specialized roles we will examine in the next chapter.

NOTE

1. Robert H. Schuller, *Your Church Has Real Possibilities* (Glendale, Calif.: Regal Books Division, G/L Publications: 1974), 49.

Chapter Thirteen

Key Roles:
Pastor and Staff

The general leadership roles within the church may be summarized by the authority roles of elders and the serving roles of deacons that we reviewed in the last chapter. In the next two chapters, I want to look with you at the specialized roles of *pastor*, *staff*, and *laity*. These terms are used more often than they are clearly understood. And though their definitions may vary among churches, the emphasis here has to do with maintaining the clarity and purpose of each role.

The title *pastor-teacher* is used in Scripture to refer to those gifted to shepherd God's people with a primary emphasis on teaching. This person is admonished in Scripture to "equip the saints for the work of ministry" (Ephesians 4:12 NRSV). With this responsibility in mind, I like to refer to the pastor as a leader-equipper. If the health of the local church is going to be measured by the degree to which believers become mature and equipped followers of Jesus Christ, then someone has to be responsible to insure that the objective is accomplished. Leading and equipping are to be among the pastor's primary responsibilities.

EQUIPPING

The word *equipping* has important biblical roots (see Ephesians 4:11–12). As it relates to a church and the pastor's role, *equipping* is used in at least three different ways. The first I call the "traditional view."

The Traditional View

Those who have this perspective see the role of the pastor and staff as paid professionals who do whatever jobs are needed. If the church needs teaching, hire a teacher. If the church needs evangelism to be accomplished, hire an evangelist. And if the church needs pastoring, hire a pastor. Unfortunately, we are all too familiar with this less-than-biblical perspective.

The Evangelical View

The second understanding of equipping I call the "evangelical view." This perspective sees the role of the pastor and staff as first, to help the church members discover their spiritual gifts (special abilities given by God's grace to enhance the work of God's kingdom), and second, to start needed ministries within the church and community. Then, last, it is their responsibility to recruit the appropriately gifted people to the appropriate ministry.

"The evangelical view" sounds pretty good, doesn't it? Not from my perspective! Most who have actually tried to put this view into practice agree with me. This approach reminds me of the circus act where the performer comes out with a stack of plates and begins spinning them on sticks stationed on the floor. By the time the tenth plate or so is up and spinning, the first is beginning to wobble. The performer races back to the first and revs up every stick until all are safely in motion again, allowing him to set plates eleven through twenty spinning. From that point on he frantically runs from plate to plate giving each stick just enough attention to keep the whole precarious arrangement spinning. So goes the life of a pastor who lives out this second approach. A vacation could be disastrous.

Years ago a man and his wife moved to Atlanta and began attending our church. He had been a successful pastor and his wife had experienced a full life as the first lady of their church. He had now taken a position with a parachurch organization in Atlanta. The wife was an attractive and very gifted woman—as well equipped for ministry as any woman in our congregation at that time. I assumed they were happy campers in our church until the day I got a stinging letter from her, filled with expressions of hurt, disappointment, and anger. She explained that the past two years of her life in Atlanta had been the first in her adult life that she had no ministry. She went on to reveal the cause of her plight by pointing a finger at me. According to her, I was guilty of gross negligence because I, as the senior pastor, had never personally given her a ministry. She apparently embraced this "evangelical view" of equipping, and I had offended and disappointed her. She had waited two years for the "spin" that never came. As a result, she explained, she and her husband had decided to leave our church.

I wrote her a gracious letter (as I do to all people who choose to express directly to me their disappointment with me or with the church). Since she had mentioned in her letter the church they would begin attending, I asked her to do herself and her new pastor (a personal friend of mine) a favor—to realize that she didn't need her pastor's permission to do ministry. God had already given it. I encouraged her to go to her pastor if she needed equipping or help in doing ministry, but never to think that God must speak through her pastor in order to legitimize her ministry.

The Biblical View

This leads us to the third view. The last approach to pastoral ministry I call the "biblical view" of equipping. Those who hold this perspective believe that the pastor and staff's responsibility is to help the church's members discover their spiritual gifts, but then to simply create an environment where God's voice can be heard. Since we embrace this view, we encourage the people of Perimeter to seek God for His leading in ministry and then, if they need help discerning that leading or need equipping to perform that ministry, to call upon us.

The Greek word translated "to equip" is *katartizo* and carries the idea of coming alongside as one seeks to arrive at his destiny—not to pull "sitters" off the bench. The perspective that members have regarding equipping will dictate their expectations and shape their involvement in the church. Only God knows accurately what ministry is best for each of His children.

WHO DOES WHAT?

Many of you reading this book probably know more about business than you do about church organization. So allow me to illustrate from your world. A business always knows who its customers, employees, and employers are. But I believe most church members don't know who takes these roles in the church. Do you? I ask this question to each monthly Inquirer's Class, which spends a weekend investigating the life of our church. When I ask who the church's customer is, I repeatedly hear a variety of answers—nonmembers, seekers, other believers—and a lot of uncertainty even in those whose responses are accurate. Then I suggest that, since we don't have agreement, we move along to the role of employee.

When I ask who they think serves in the church in a role comparable to the employee within a business, you could guess the answers. Some would say, staff members; others, church members; and others, ordained pastors. Only when I ask whom they see functioning in the role of employer do I get unanimity in response. Everyone agrees that God is the employer—until I ask them who the owner is. Of course, I explain that within a business you may well have an owner and employer being the same person, so technically they are right. But, assuming a four-tier organization as listed below, I ask them to begin at the top with God as the owner and to work down, seeking to determine who fulfills the roles of the other three.

Owner	=	God
Employer	=	_____
Employee	=	_____
Customer	=	_____

At this point people usually agree that the staff (after I explain that they serve with the elders and under their authority) serve in the role of employer. The members of the church, they agree, occupy the role of employee. Then, when all agree that the unchurched are our customers, I explain that church members are also our customers because we are also called to minister to one another.

Now, look at the filled-in blanks below and answer the question, Whose responsibility is it to reach the customer? The answer, employee, becomes obvious. So what is the role of the employer? The answer: to invest in the employee in such a way as to enable that person to do his or her job adequately. This involves leading and equipping, among other things.

Owner	=	God
Employer	=	Elders/Staff
Employee	=	Members
Customer	=	Unchurched and Members

The Scriptures tell us that the same is true in the life of God's church. Ephesians 4:11–12 explains that pastor-teachers are to *equip* the saints for the work of ministry. Judged by the actual practice in most churches, you would think that God gave pastor-teachers to *do* the work of ministry. To the degree that equipping remains an optional duty and the saints become an insignificant middleman in God's design for ministry, the church will not prevail.

ACCOUNTABILITY

Keeping our business illustration in mind, imagine that I am the regional sales manager of a large company. I have just gathered my sales force for quarterly sales reports. I begin, in roll-call fashion, to call out names. "Jo Anne?"

Jo Anne responds simply, "No sales to report."

Shocked, to say the least, I show restraint and say nothing, simply moving to the next name. "John?"

As before, the response is simply, "No sales to report." Now I am flabbergasted. This is, after all, a sales report meeting! After hearing the next five employees give the same response, I look out over the audience of salesmen and women and ask, with great frustration, "Who has had any sales? Raise your hands." Not one hand goes up. Then I go ballistic and begin railing at my sales force for their laziness and irresponsibility.

In the midst of this, Scott stands up and speaks for the rest of the team. He says, "Randy, don't be so alarmed. We want you to know that we have all worked very diligently this past quarter."

I interrupt, concerned. "Oh no, I can't believe it. Our competition must have overtaken us. They've bettered our product."

Scott speaks up again and says, "No, we still have the best product in the market."

More confused, I blurt out, "Oh no, my worst fear! There's no longer a market for our product."

Again, Scott corrects me by saying, "Randy, relax. Wrong again. We have worked hard. The market is wide open and we have the best product at the lowest price."

So I throw up my hands and say, "I surrender. Help me out. I don't understand."

To this Scott says, "Randy, we have been working hard this quarter but what we've been doing is spending our time trying to come up with new and improved employee benefit plans. We've got some great ideas to suggest to you and then the management. Aren't you excited, Randy?"

To this I respond, practically screaming, "Not in the least! That's not your job."

In much of the church today, members are spending much of their time working to enhance their own employee benefits and failing to give themselves to the task of reaching the customer. This is one of the main reasons for the ineffectiveness of the church. Having read the scenario above, you might expect me to rail against lax church members. What I am going to do, however, is to address the pastor's leadership job description. Notice that I say *leadership* job description, not *pastoral* job description (which will be discussed later).

LEADERSHIP JOB DESCRIPTION

I believe that the pastor's leadership job description includes four primary responsibilities:

1. *The pastor is to spend time with the Lord discerning His leading regarding the future direction of the church.*

Quite a while ago, I read that the president of an Ivy League school said something like this: "Unless 20 percent of my time is spent with my feet on my desk, I can only manage this organization—but I cannot lead it." He was saying that he had to spend time away from the day-to-day responsibilities that robbed him of the time to think about the future.

In chapter 12, I quoted from a description of leadership that included these thoughts: "Leadership is thinking ahead, planning for the future, exhausting all possibilities, envisioning problems and dreaming up solutions to them, and then communicating the possibilities and problem-solving ideas to the decision makers."[1] In the early years of our church, the elders told me they wanted me to spend four weeks a year away from my regular responsibilities doing exactly what is described above—along with time spent talking and listening to God. I have kept this practice now for nearly twenty-five years and have never regretted the time spent away.

159

2. The leader-equipper sets goals for the church according to the will of God.

In our church polity, the elders ultimately approve our goals, but they rely on me and our staff to wrestle with the initial formation of those goals and then to make recommendations.

3. The leader-equipper obtains goal ownership from the people.

If the members do not understand or accept their role in the church, the system will break down. This is one of the most difficult assignments to accomplish in any church—especially in a large church. Finding the appropriate time and place is the issue. Doubtlessly, the most significant time to do this, for us, has been a special series of banquets offered prior to the beginning of our new ministry year. Everyone is urged to attend one of these banquets where, in addition to outstanding food, music, and drama, I share the vision and goals for the coming year of ministry. Obviously vision is cast in many different venues, but this has proven to be our most effective setting.

4. Last, the leader-equipper sees that each member of the church is properly equipped to do his or her part in accomplishing these goals.

We will say more about this in the chapter dealing with strategy.

PASTORAL JOB DESCRIPTION

So much for the pastor's leadership job description. What about his pastoral job description? Before making several observations, let me strongly suggest that the pastor's pastoral responsibilities must be limited. Let me explain.

Time and Responsibilities

Let the three circles below represent three options for a pastor who serves a church of one hundred members or more. Think about the implications. Only one hundred members can actually represent hundreds of people whose problems could ultimately necessitate the time of the pastor. For instance, if a member's parent in another state is diagnosed with cancer, the member now has a problem. If a member's next-door neighbor is depressed and needs pastoral help or is going through a divorce and needs counsel, the pastor is most likely to be asked to respond. All of a sudden, this church of one hundred members represents hundreds of people who may need the pastor on any given day. And the larger the church, the more accentuated the problem.

Now, let's develop the details of these circles. Each circle represents a twenty-four-hour day. The first circle refers to the pastor who spends most of his time responding to pastoral needs. The large P stands for pastoral responsibilities. The letter E, a combination of an L and an E, represents the tasks of leading and equipping. Notice how little attention is given to this role—and understandably so. Something must go to leave time for one's personal life, represented by the small inner circle (includes family time, time for personal worship, leisure, physical exercise, sleep). The bad news is that this pastor fails to lead and equip the people to do the work of ministry. The good news is that the pastor stays relatively sane.

I have never been guilty of living in the first circle, but I am much too personally familiar with circle number two. The second circle represents the pastor whose entire life is filled with church, both pastoring and leading and equipping. Unfortunately, the personal life gets pushed aside. I am amazed how many pastors lose their kids as a result of the failure to spend adequate time with them. It's also common to find pastors out of physical condition and spending little time in personal worship. And to make it worse, these imbalances are often excused and praised as evidence of hard work and faithfulness to the call of God.

Please don't misinterpret my next comments about the time constraints pastors face. Those in my profession have no corner of ownership on time pressure and fatigue. Pastors for the most part don't work longer hours than many business leaders. But pastors do work different hours than those in the marketplace (which is neither better nor worse). Many laypeople have to leave for work five days a week at six o'clock in the morning and don't return home until seven in the evening. Yet I can manage my schedule so as to take off work in the midafternoon, if I choose. I have often been the only male parent at a child's ball practice. What an advantage! On the other hand, it is not unusual for me to work thirty of my weekly hours outside the traditional work times of eight to five, Monday through Friday. Much of my work has to be done in early morning and night meetings and weekend activities. The issue is not one of when does one work, but of whether or not one's work robs a person of his higher priorities.

It has not been uncommon through the years for one of my children to ask me in the morning whether or not I would be home that night. More often than not my response has been, "No." However, I have also been able to say, "But I will be home at three this afternoon and will play with you till dinnertime."

On many occasions, immediately prior to this important hour, as I'm packing up to leave the office, my secretary will hand me a few "important" phone messages. On the one hand, I have church members who expect me to call immediately. On the other hand, I have a child who needs me at home. What do I do? Unfortunately, too often in the early years of ministry, I would reluctantly go to the phone and return those calls—and far too often have to return home later than scheduled only to seek forgiveness from my child.

Do you know why I made such unwise choices? Because I am insecure. I love the approval of my peers. My reasoning at the time was, *I know these people. God calls them His sheep and they are, but I have learned all too well that sheep bite tenaciously. On the other hand, my child is so gracious, and I know he or she will understand.* Here's the danger, however.

Though the child may be sweet now, he may express his displeasure in profound ways at sixteen or seventeen years of age. A little child may repeatedly understand and forgive a parent's insensitivity and inconsistencies, but a child will not know what to do with the hurt that remains even after forgiveness. If that hurt accumulates enough, it will eventually spill over into shocking results.

Through the years I have learned that the same sheep who would bite me if I didn't meet their need upon request are the very ones who would say, if my child rebelled, "If anyone should model the family, it's the pastor. He should have spent more time with his children." The way I look at it, if I'm going to be criticized one way or the other, why not do so while keeping my kids on my team?

The circle on the far right represents the balanced life of a pastor who applies Ephesians 4:11–12 to his ministry. His primary task is to equip the saints, yet he does keep an appropriate time allotted in his life for pastoral and personal responsibilities.

Responsibilities

So in what ways does the pastor manage his pastoral responsibilities? I suggest that the pastor's pastoral job description is composed of four primary responsibilities:

1. To shepherd the staff
2. To shepherd the elders
3. To shepherd personal friends in crisis
4. To shepherd every person in need who makes their needs known when no one else is equipped yet to minister to them

Notice that the solution never involves allowing people's genuine needs to go unmet so that the pastor can maintain attention to his own well-being. If I, as a pastor, have not equipped anyone to meet a particular person's needs, then it becomes my job. The greater the number of needs or roles in the church that only the pastor can meet, the more evidence exists that the pastor is failing to equip enough people to do the work of the ministry.

Costs

Last, for pastors and staff members to maintain their appropriate job description, they must be willing to pay the following costs.

1. To assume responsibility for failure.

Remember the story in chapter 3 of Bear Bryant when he rebuked Bill Curry for his lack of assuming responsibility for failure? "If anything goes bad, I did it." Good leaders take responsibility for the failure of the organization they lead. Enough said.

2. To major on his primary responsibilities.

The pastor must pay the cost of sticking to that which God has called him, regardless of what fellow man expects of him.

3. To share his ministry responsibility with the laity.

Many pastors do not want to share the pastoral responsibilities because nothing invites the accolades and approval of members like pastoring them in their time of need. Do so and they will support you and love you for the rest of your ministry. On the other hand, equip people to do the ministry and you may not get even as much as a "Thank-you" from those whose needs have been met.

The cost of sticking to your guns is high, but so are the benefits. A healthy and humbling satisfaction occurs when someone you have equipped is highly praised for his or her ministry. God's kingdom is richly blessed, and thus the King of the kingdom is honored.

We will explore some of the details of these costs in the next chapter, as we examine the role of the laity.

NOTE

1. Robert H. Schuller, *Your Church Has Real Possibilities* (Glendale, Calif.: Regal Books Division, G/L Publications, 1974), 49.

Chapter Fourteen

꧁꧂

Key Roles:
Laity

The expression "Every member a minister" has gained wide popularity among churches. We use it frequently at Perimeter. But we have also been reminded that a description is less than an accomplishment. Many churches that print the claim "Every member a minister" on their weekly bulletin would be hard-pressed to describe what that phrase actually means. The first Reformation gave the *Word* of God back to the people of God. Today we need a second Reformation that gives the *work* of God back to the people of God. That will not happen until the laity accept their role as ministers.

The only way the pastor and staff of a church can fulfill their rightful job descriptions is for the laity to fulfill theirs. The roles are inseparable and interdependent. Like two sides of a coin, one cannot exist without the other.

LAITY JOB DESCRIPTION

Four primary responsibilities ought to be included in a biblically oriented job description for the laypersons in the church:

1. To discover and develop their spiritual gifts.

Every church ought to have a vehicle to systematically introduce believers to the teaching of God's Word regarding spiritual gifts. The availability of these tools has greatly enhanced the possibility of equipping, but not if they are left unused.

2. To view themselves as the primary ministers of the church.

That phrase is almost as easy to say as "Every member a minister." The truth is that the laity will not see themselves in this way until the leadership in the church persistently sees them that way. The laity should be considered the primary ministers of the church and must be willing to deliberately lay claim to that role. Perhaps the following story will illustrate how the transition can take place.

Joe's Story

Joe and his family had moved to Atlanta from Alabama. Joe and Catherine had three children, a daughter in high school and two junior-high-age sons. Because this family had been active members of a Protestant church, Joe assumed he was a believer. But constant exposure to God's Word and God's people revealed to him otherwise. By the age of forty, Joe was already a successful businessman. Both his feet were firmly planted in the middle of the world's values.

But when he met Christ in a life-transforming way, everything he stood for began to change. In a sense, he took a step into the kingdom of God and his weight shifted irreversibly toward eternity. One foot, however, was still stuck in his previous way of living. During that time period, Joe could have easily been compared to the Corinthians addressed by Paul in 1 Corinthians 3. He was still "fleshy . . . walking like mere men"

(v. 3). Joe's new life was under construction, but not without the trials and problems God often uses as the instruments of purging.

Meanwhile, Joe's daughter Jessica graduated from high school. She had been not only a spiritual leader but also quite popular. She was selected to be both a cheerleader and the homecoming queen, all the while maintaining a reputation as a young person who took God seriously. When she graduated from high school, she went on to the University of Alabama.

Only a few weeks into her freshman year, Jessica was killed in a car wreck. As could be imagined, Joe's heart was pierced through and through. In the midst of the pain of this human tragedy, Joe sensed his dragging foot, previously caught in the attachments of this world, begin to loosen. After all, a big part of his reason for interest in this world was now in the next—and his heart followed.

WE NEED TO GIVE THE WORK OF GOD
BACK TO THE PEOPLE OF GOD!

Soon after Jessica's tragic death, Joe found out he had inoperable and terminal cancer. He underwent chemotherapy treatment, but the powerful drugs were only able to slow down the disease. Faced with the reality of a shortened life expectancy (outside a supernatural healing of God), Joe's back foot, until then caught up in the world's priorities, lifted and swung freely into the realm of eternal pursuit. After all, what did the world have to offer him now? (By the way, how often do you think about the fact that we are all dying right now and that everyone we love will also die one day? Why do we keep senselessly investing in the things of this world?)

Even as his body deteriorated, Joe experienced accelerated spiritual growth. His past lifestyle, by choice and by doctor's orders, changed radically. He had to cease the day-to-day responsibilities of his occupation.

His fast-paced life shifted into low gear. Suddenly, Joe had a lot of immediate time on his hands and little reason to worry about long-term plans. At this point he was still mobile, driving his car and doing basic daily functions, caring for his family.

Pause

I will temporarily put the story of Joe on pause here for a moment. From time to time, especially in the early years of our church, I received calls from pastors of churches outside of Atlanta telling me of members of their churches who were in Atlanta receiving special medical treatment at Emory Hospital. These pastors would ask if I could be their members' pastor while they were in Atlanta, visiting them and ministering to them as often as possible. Unbeknownst to these pastors, such a visit from where I live would take the better part of a half day. Unable to meet this need personally, I nevertheless have always responded by saying, "I can't promise you that I will minister to them, but I can assure you that I'll have someone who is adequately equipped do so."

One pastor responded to this answer by saying, "Well, if it's not an ordained clergy, don't waste their time. My member will not accept the ministry of someone not ordained." Can you believe it? Those church members don't even know me! That pastor greatly underestimated the power of peer ministry. Many of our laity are far more gifted and qualified to do pastoral care work than I am.

In fact, I freely admit that if someone needs pastoral care and gets me as their pastor, compared to these other more gifted laymen, they get ripped off! Though I know I have the heart of a pastor, I don't have many of the gifts related to crisis pastoral care. I don't hold hands well with people when they hurt. I don't cry well with those who cry. I could go on and on. God did not give me the gift of mercy. When I walk into a hospital room and see a tube in someone's throat, my first response may well be not to express empathy, but to question whether it is really needed!

Many years ago, I used to visit every woman in our church who had a baby. Not only did this create much work for me, but very stressful work at that! I know this may sound odd to you, but figuratively speaking, I would drive around the hospital parking lot several times, mustering up the courage to perform my obligation. Perhaps you are thinking, *Grow up, Randy. How can you be hesitating over the easiest and most pleasant kind of hospital visit?*

But my response to those who would think this way is as follows. How would you feel if someone gave you an assignment of having lunch with someone you have never met, with the specific purpose of sharing Christ with him? Assume that you are told that this person is intellectually more capable than you and, in fact, a near-genius. You also discover that this person is rude and downright mean, expressing hatred toward Christians and always looking for a good debate to put down Christianity. I imagine that some of you reading this would perhaps, figuratively speaking, drive around the restaurant parking lot several times before going in— if you even went in at all. Do you know my first response to such avoidance? "Grow up." You see, God has made me in such a way that when I have that challenge facing me at the end of the week, I wake up each morning counting down the days to this upcoming highlight of my ministry week.

The point is that God has gifted us all differently, and we must respect and work according to these differences. What I see in church after church are multitudes of God's people with amazing gifts for ministry sitting idle while a handful of "professionals" try to do too much of what they are not particularly gifted to do. We need to give the work of God back to the people of God!

Back to Joe's Story

About this time in Joe's spiritual odyssey, I received a request to visit a man who was a patient at Emory, and I gave my typical response.

The relieved pastor said, "Fine. Thank you for any help you can offer."

I asked a little about his member's history and character, looking for some insight that might help me assign the right person to minister to him. When I was told that this man was dying of cancer and was taking chemotherapy, I immediately thought of Joe as my potential ministry candidate. I called Joe to ask if he could help me. He graciously volunteered to help in any way that he could. I explained to Joe that I needed him to go to Emory and be a minister to a man dying of cancer.

Joe's immediate response was to say that he would have no idea how to perform such a ministry. I explained that his lack of preparation was my fault because I am an equipper of the saints and I had failed to do my job! I asked if he would agree to do his job as a minister on the condition that I would first do mine as the equipper. He agreed.

After giving Joe some simple equipping and encouragement on what to do and how to perform his ministry, I sent him on his way to Emory. Later that day Joe rushed into my office and exclaimed, "Randy, you told me this man was dying, but you didn't tell me that he's probably going to die in the next few days and that he's not a believer. Randy, you've got to get to that hospital and witness to him before he dies."

I hope that by now my response won't surprise you. I said, "Joe, did you know you don't have to be ordained to share the gospel?"

He responded, "I have no idea how to share the gospel." I explained, once again, that that was my fault. I am an equipper and had failed to equip him for one of life's most important responsibilities as a believer. I asked if he would be willing to do his job on the condition that I would be willing to do my job. He reluctantly agreed.

After a crash course on sharing his faith, Joe made his way back to Emory. He shared the gospel with this man and visited him daily until the man died.

Now there's no story of salvation to report, but Joe's response was significant. Catching me outside the auditorium after a service, Joe said to me, "Randy, I've been thinking and have come to the conclusion that you should never go to hospitals to do pastoral work."

I asked him to explain.

He answered, "Be honest. How many times would you have visited this man with cancer? Once?"

I agreed.

He said, "That's all that could be expected of you. There's one of you and many sick people. But for me, no one expects me to do pastoral work at the hospital. So I can concentrate on one person and give him more attention than you could."

I agreed.

Then he added in his own humorous but sincere way, "And besides, I think I probably did a better job than you could have done!" I loved hearing this and was delighted by how this experience had impacted his life.

But this story has one more chapter. Not long after this episode, I got a call from Joe. I heard concern in his tone of voice and asked what the problem was. He explained that he had just received a phone call from his thirty-eight-year-old neighbor. This young man's wife had dropped dead, apparently of a heart attack, while in their kitchen cooking with her two young daughters. The shattered husband was in shock and uncertain what to do. He told Joe that just the week before he and his wife had been driving along talking about Jessica's funeral—how unique and celebratory it had been.

During that conversation they had also briefly discussed their own situation. Since neither of them had a church or a pastor, they wondered what they would do if something happened to one of them. The wife said to her husband, "If I die before you, I'd like for you to see if Joe's pastor is still in Atlanta. And if he is, I would like him to do my funeral." Little did either of them realize that this would be perhaps her final request. With those words in mind, this man had called Joe to ask him to call me to see if I would be his pastor during his time of need.

Joe said to me, "Randy, I know you can't do everyone's friend's funeral, but in light of the uniqueness of this situation, would you be willing to be this family's pastor?"

To this I responded, "Joe, did you know that you don't have to be ordained to do funerals?" Joe did everything but drop the phone. He knew what was coming. He said, "Oh no! Hospital visitation and witnessing, yes, but not funerals. No way."

My honest reply to Joe was that I could not do it but would consider it my job to equip him to meet that need. Joe was beside himself. He knew I was serious. Eventually, I compromised and told Joe I would strike a deal with him. I offered to do half the funeral and pastoral work if he would do the other half with me. I assured him that I would equip him to do his part. Once again, he reluctantly agreed.

You've never seen a more nervous man than Joe when he showed up at the funeral home for the service. But when all was said and done, though I perhaps was the more articulate speaker, without question Joe was the more effective minister. The reason is obvious—I didn't know this family. But Joe loved them and genuinely shared their pain.

Everyone needs such people in their lives. If a church grows as it should, one person could never be that close a friend to every member. And besides, even if he could, there would be no time to adequately equip the saints to do the work of ministry. If the pastor can (or thinks he can) do everything, why should the laity feel compelled to do anything?

Now to the third responsibility of the laymen's job description.

3. To spend the time needed to be equipped adequately to use their spiritual gifts.

Gifts take time to develop. Much effort must be invested in learning to steward these gifts well so as to maximize one's impact with their usage.

4. To commit the time necessary to use their gifts in ministry.

To have the necessary gifts and even to be proficient in their usage is of no value if there is no time available to put them to use. Time must be scheduled for such.

COSTS

Having described the responsibilities that are part of the job description of the laymen in the church, we now look at the costs laymen must be willing to pay in order to make all of this work. Jesus had some pointed things to say about the importance of counting costs before embarking on discipleship (Luke 14:25–33). There are at least three:

1. To allow the pastor and staff to be equippers.

It is not good enough to endorse the principle and then to hold one-self out as the exception to the rule. We must encourage our pastor and staff to be equippers. A congregation requires a great deal of patient train-ing to reach this understanding. The old habits of direct pastoral care resist change. Wise laypeople go out of their way to encourage equipping efforts undertaken by their pastor and staff.

2. To readjust fellowship and leisure habits.

This relates to making time available. Some believers have their dis-cretionary time so filled with fellowship activities, Bible study groups, hobbies, and sports that there is no time available to serve other people in their time of need. We certainly want others to be free to come to our aid during our times of crises. So, likewise, we have to make the time available to be ministers to our friends in need. Believers need to be trained by their leader's example and teaching to maintain a clear dis-tinction between busyness and effectiveness.

3. To follow God-ordained leadership with an attitude of trust.

The elders and staff give overall direction to the ministry in which laymen are called to serve. Without an attitude of submission on the part of the laity, the service rendered will always be selective, dependent upon the degree of agreement with that overall direction.

Analogy: Marriage

Perhaps the analogy of marriage serves to illustrate this point best. I realize that one of the most debated issues in the church today in-volves the role of women in church and marriage. I am a strong propo-nent of the historical, biblical teaching that clearly delineates different roles for men and women in marriage and the church. I realize that admitting such may cause many to stop reading at this point (thus my strategy of putting this toward the end). Since you are still reading, let me ask you not to jump to conclusions too quickly!

Unfortunately, most people seem to think that since the divided biblical roles designate the man as the "head" and the women as the "submissive one," therefore man has the superior role and the woman the inferior one. This could not be further from the truth. Why is it that we assume such? After all, Jesus, the second person of the Trinity, has for all eternity been "the same in substance, equal in power and glory" to the Father, as the Westminster Longer Catechism puts it. Jesus' divine, intrinsic worth did not change when He became incarnate and voluntarily took on a role of submission. In fact, isn't it interesting that the "equal party" of the Trinity, who humbled Himself by living in submission to His equal, is the very One who, while remaining equal, is now "exalted as head over all" (1 Chronicles 29:11 NIV; see also Philippians 2:5–11)?

This is not intended to be an exposition of the biblical view of the role of men and women in marriage. I am simply laying a foundation in order to illustrate the above point about the impact of submission in the life of the church. Imagine with me that Suzanne is married to Brad. A decision has to be made regarding an issue on which Brad and Suzanne have not been able to reach agreement. Extended conversations, debates, arguments, and even compromise have failed to settle the issue. Repeated tie votes have only demonstrated that democracy doesn't work in marriage. According to my understanding of the biblical teaching regarding roles, Brad has the ultimate responsibility to make the final decision. After all, to not make a decision in certain situations is to make a decision (for example, "Do we sell our house?").

Though it is God's design for the man to have the responsibility to make the decision, that arrangement does not suggest that his views are always accurate or even the best ones. For instance, I am the head of our house, but I *often* decide to do what Carol thinks is best. No, it's not what you're thinking—that I'm the head but my wife is the neck that turns it! I serve in the role or capacity of a player-coach. It's my job to put the best batter up to the plate. Sometimes I put Carol up to the plate (go with her decision though in disagreement with my best judgment) and let her bat. I do this because I realize that she has a better batting average than I do in certain areas of decision making. At other times I step up to the plate (go with my decision), believing I have a better batting average in such situations.

Assuming this view of the Bible's teaching on roles in marriage, let's go back to Brad and Suzanne's impasse. Suppose in this particular situation, Brad goes with his own judgment, though it contradicts Suzanne's absolute confidence that Brad is making the wrong decision. What are Suzanne's options now that the decision has been made?

LIFE WITHIN A LOCAL BODY OF CHRIST OFFERS PLENTY OF OPPORTUNITIES FOR THE PRACTICE OF MUTUAL SUBMISSION

As I see it, she has three options, only one of which is biblical. First, she could say, "Brad, if the decision you have made ends up being wrong, as I'm absolutely sure it will, I will divorce you. In fact, I'm beginning proceedings immediately." Resorting to a parting of ways is an option, but not a biblical one.

Second, Suzanne could respond, "Brad, you know that I don't think you are doing the right thing by making that decision, but even if I am right and you are wrong, I would never even so much as think about divorce. However, you will wish that I had divorced you!" Again, threatening retaliation or punishment is an option, but not a biblical one.

The third option for Suzanne is to say, "Brad, I honestly wish you wouldn't make that decision, but I realize that a decision has to be made. I'm glad you're willing to take that responsibility. I'm still on your team and we'll work through the problems that result if you are wrong."

Notice I never so much as suggested the option of saying, "Brad, what do I know about what's best? I'm just a woman and you, the superior one, must know best what to do." It makes me nauseous even to write these words! More often than not, a woman who wisely responds to her husband's decisions in a biblical fashion often discovers that her husband suddenly wants to check to make sure he has listened clearly to her reasons.

Back to the Church

Likewise, in the church, laymen's views are valuable and as often right as wrong. Laymen should never be taught that they should remain quiet without strongly expressing their opinions about the direction of their church's ministry. But neither should it be an option to divorce God's church over disagreements about decisions made. (Please note that I don't believe that changing churches equates to divorcing the church. But changing churches over disagreements may be unwise and often indicates a lack of willingness to submit to God-given authority. By using the term *divorce* I am referring to terminating relationship with God's organized family over the decision of one church.)

Unfortunately, many churchmen routinely choose the second option in their relationship with the church. They resent decisions that don't go their way. They proudly express their determination to "stick it out" while carefully nursing their anger, hurt, and bitterness. It often becomes their mission to make life miserable for the leadership of God's church. God abhors such attitudes (Proverbs 6:16–19). To say the least, it's a sad commentary on the selfish condition of so many true believers.

It is the third option that God has called His family to take. It is a humble option. But God exalts the humble and gives grace to those who practice healthy submission within the church. Life within a local body of Christ offers plenty of opportunities for the practice of mutual submission (Ephesians 5:21). It is amazing to think of the potential unleashed in the family of God when each elder, deacon, pastor, staff member, and layperson not only discovers and implements the use of his or her spiritual gifts, but uses those gifts in the role to which God has called him or her. Clarifying such roles or job descriptions will ultimately be a blessing to God's people and an advantage in the advancement of His kingdom.

Chapter Fifteen

——∞∞∞——

Seventh Component of
an Effective Ministry Plan:
A STRATEGICALLY DESIGNED
INFRASTRUCTURE

W hen I was a child, we sometimes played a game called Mr.
Potato Head. Perhaps it's still being played today. But in
case you're not familiar with it, let me tell you how it works.
You begin with a bare plastic potato that functions as a head. On
one side of the potato you find two holes where the eyes should
be and one hole each in the place of the mouth and nose. Included in the game box are several different sets of eyes and ears
and several different noses and mouths. It's intriguing how different that potato head face can look depending upon what combination is used.

For many years at our annual staff retreat we played a similar game with the infrastructure of our church. In fact, we called
it Mr. Potato Head. The holes in the potato head represented the
prime times in the life of the church (Sunday morning being
number one). The facial pieces represented the components of

our infrastructure defined by our "what we do" values. By visualizing our suggested changes and priorities in this way, we were able not only to laugh at ourselves at times but also to discover some new looks for our ministry structure.

As mentioned earlier, outside the work of God's Spirit and the groundwork of consistent prayer, there are three main resources necessary to make a specific ministry more likely to succeed—primary leadership, primary financial resources, and prime time. Designing a ministry infrastructure has to do with determining which functions in the life of the church get prime time and primary leadership. (By the way, typically financial resources will follow prime time and primary leadership.)

Many questions need to be answered as we examine an existing infrastructure and propose changes. Will the church use Sunday morning as a time to worship, to reach nonbelievers, or to do both? Will the church be centralized or decentralized for most of its ministries? Will the church have a midweek centralized worship service or prayer meeting, or will it concentrate on decentralized groups throughout the week? And if the congregation is decentralized into small groups, will they be designed as discipleship groups or merely as care, share, and Bible study groups? Will Sunday night be used to gather again for worship, and if so, will it be an alternative service from that offered on Sunday morning or will it merely be a repeat service? Or will Sunday night be viewed as a time for all of God's people to slow down and enjoy their day of rest?

And then, what about specialized needs, such as youth and children? When will they meet and for what functions? Will the youth meet as a segregated ministry or will the ministry be structured as a pure cell church where youth, children, and adults stay together within the context of ministry? When these questions, along with many related ones, have been dealt with adequately, you have defined your infrastructure.

Every culture, and even community within a specific culture, defines its own prime time. The number one prime time for church activities in America differs from that in Japan. Suburbanites in North Atlanta define their number one prime time differently than the Bohemians in the same city do. It is important that the congregation's use of prime time lines up consistently with the church's previously determined "what we do" values.

This is exactly what seeker service churches have done so well. They have set outreach as their highest "what we do" value and aligned it with their number one prime time, Sunday morning.

Allow me to suggest a caution, however, at this point. Be certain that a decision not to align worship with the Lord's Day is not a compromise of your biblical theology merely for the sake of practical functionality. It is not my intention to argue any position regarding the use of the Lord's Day or, for that matter, the priority of worship versus outreach. The rule must always be that God's Word is our infallible directive.

HOW WILL WE STRUCTURE OUR ORGANIZATION SO THAT WE CAN ACCOMPLISH OUR MISSION?

In reality, what we are doing when we design a church's infrastructure is answering this question. Up to this point, we have been discussing infrastructure as it relates to values. There are other issues that shape one's choices in structuring a church. Issues such as one's perspective regarding how size impacts the health of the church, or how sociological, social, and spiritual needs dictate the type of ministry offerings a church should provide are just a few. Permit me to share some insights and observations that relate to these issues.

Size: "Large" Is OK

Let's first consider the issue of size. How often have we heard disparaging statements about large churches? One of the widely held assumptions is that large churches are unfriendly. I'd like to challenge this notion, albeit with a smile. In fact, I have a suspicion that if this criticism is leveled accurately at any church at all, it should be leveled against the small church. This may, in part, account for why some churches remain small.

While vacationing one summer on the Florida coast, our family visited a small church in the community where we were staying. The church

179

had a great reputation regarding its theological orthodoxy, but beyond this, I knew nothing about it. Because we didn't know what attire would be appropriate, we played conservative—the guys dressed in coat and tie and the girls put on dresses. Not certain about the worship service time, we arrived at 10:30 A.M. We misjudged on the side of caution in both ways—the dress was casual dress and the starting time was 11:00 A.M.

As we entered the building, we found that the foyer served as a fellowship hall. We had to walk through a roomful of people to enter the small sanctuary. They were having coffee and "fellowship." It was obvious we were guests, if for no other reason than the six of us were the only people "dressed up" for the service. We immediately noticed that though people were looking over at us, no one approached to welcome us.

CELEBRATION IS ONE ACTIVITY
OF THE LOCAL CHURCH
THAT HAS POTENTIAL
TO GET MORE DYNAMIC
THE LARGER IT BECOMES

I decided to have some fun. I told Carol and the kids to stay by the door we had entered, and I took a stroll. I circled the room looking quickly from right to left, pretending to be looking for something. I was curious to see if I could provoke someone to be friendly or to ask if I needed help. If successful, I was going to ask for a bulletin. But my mission failed. When I arrived back at the starting point, I told Carol and the kids to follow me into the sanctuary. We walked through the middle of the crowd, took our seats, and waited twenty minutes or so as others took their seats. We left when the service was over, without ever being welcomed. So much for the claim that small churches are just naturally friendly! Certainly, I know that many small churches are friendly and many large churches unfriendly. But the reverse is also true. In my opinion, we have nabbed the wrong villain. The culprit behind unfriendliness is not size but structure.

The Structure Villain

Most churches begin as small churches. The small inner circle below can illustrate them. Within this small group flows excellent social engagement and community. Due to attractive programs, good preaching, or just simply the grace of God alone, the church begins to grow (illustrated by the exterior circles). The core, however, tends to remain a closed group. There's a certain practicality mixed with pride that assumes only members of the original group are qualified to be the keepers and guardians of the flame. Since most churches are structured in a centralized manner, people enter the outer life of the church through the large group gatherings. Most newcomers find it difficult, if not impossible, to break into the core group.

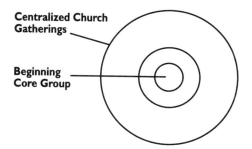

Let me describe a healthier structure. Assume the church to be a collection of small groups (illustrated on the next page by the small circles). These groups may be discipleship groups, prayer groups, service groups, neighborhood groups—whatever. Each week new groups are being started. These become important attraction and entry points for new people. Then, each week, the people from all these small groups gather collectively to worship (illustrated by the outer circle). Worship is a celebration. The good news is that celebration is one activity of the local church that has potential to get more dynamic the larger it becomes.

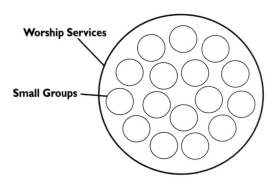

Analogy: Baseball Thrills

Can you imagine being a fanatic Atlanta Braves fan in 1991? You have cheered your team to first place from last place the year before. You've been waiting for this day as long as you can remember. You are privileged to be at the last game of the National League playoffs. You are sitting with your best friend and fellow maniac fan, George. If Atlanta wins, it goes to the World Series.

It's the bottom of the ninth, score tied. A run means a victory for Atlanta. Cabrarra is up to bat, and Sid Bream is on second. Ironically, the go-ahead runner has only one good leg. The outfield is playing in. The pitch is delivered. Cabrarra swings. The sweet crack of the bat echoes and the ball sails over the shortstop's outstretched glove. The left fielder makes a clean pickup after one hop, even as the third base coach is frantically waving Bream around third. The throw whistles toward the catcher "on a rope"! The ball and Bream will arrive at home plate at the exact same moment. Bream slides. The tag sweeps across his body. It is a photo finish. Every eye is on the home plate umpire. An instant of silence settles on the stadium. And then, after what seems to be a little longer than forever, the umpire sweeps open his arms to declare Bream safe—and the Braves are on their way to the World Series.

The home crowd erupts in celebration. Cokes and beers spill; high fives, hugs, and jubilant shouts are delivered. People are kissing folks they have never met. As you and fifty-three thousand others stand, you turn to George to celebrate with a high five. That's when you realize George is still sitting in his chair—emotionless. You shout at him, "George, George, did you miss what happened? We won! We're going to the big one!" Yet George remains quiet and reserved, simply nodding in agreement. You ask, "What's the matter, George?"

Can you imagine him replying, "There are just too many people here to celebrate"? Of course not. In fact, usually, the bigger the crowd, the easier it is to lose oneself in celebration.

What we illustrated by the passing fortune of a sports team is infinitely true of genuine worship. There are never too many people to celebrate the worth of God. My observation has been that, normally, as worship resources develop and expand in a church, there is also a heightened freedom to celebrate, making worship all the richer.

Certainly, I am not saying that the only reason for a centralized gathering of the church is for weekend worship services. But I am lobbying for the leadership of churches to consider what can be done best by the centralized church and what can be done better by the decentralized congregation. Such an evaluation will go a long way toward developing a healthy infrastructure.

Before I leave the issue of size, let me say a word about the size of small groups as it relates to function. A good rule of thumb is to remember that *social needs* are best defined by *group size*, whereas *maturity needs* are best defined by *group function*. In other words, if we want a newcomer in the church to be able to make much-needed social relationships, we put that person in a group large enough to have many options of new friends. Hopefully, that will allow him or her to find a few people who fit well as potential new friends. (And, by the way, the more evenly mixed male and female, the better.) But if we want to help someone grow deeply toward maturity in Christ, we want to put that person in a small group, no bigger than seven or eight. Such discipleship groups work best when gender specific—men with men and women with women.

Form and Function

Years ago, much was being made of the necessity of believers to find in their church an infrastructure described by three words—*cell, congregation,* and *celebration.* These terms referred to a small group of five to seven, a midsized group of thirty to sixty, and then a group as large as you pleased for celebration.

My opinion is that such terms are misleading and miss the point. They suggest that if people find all three in their church (for example, a small group, a Sunday school class, and a worship gathering) their basic needs will be met. Not so. The terms speak of form but fail to address the bigger need, function.

I suggest we replace these three words with the following terms (or similar ones) that address the real needs of our people.

Celebration—a daily personal and weekly corporate worship encounter with God

Community—supportive, accountable relationships with other believers

Class—a structured plan for understanding and applying the Word of God

Commission—an engagement with nonkingdom people with the intent of introducing them to Christ

When a Christian finds these functions taking place in his life, you can be certain that he is making advancement in his spiritual pilgrimage.

Since I have already tipped my hand regarding the value I place on discipleship, you might suspect that I would lobby strongly for an infrastructure designed around a healthy worship experience and small groups that are discipleship-oriented. Keep in mind that when I use the term *discipleship,* I am not using it in the broadest sense but in a more narrow use. I am referring to equipped leaders who labor in the life of a few to the end of imparting not only the truth of God's Word but also the substance of their lives (1 Thessalonians 2:8). We will address this subject more specifically in chapter 21.

Now, hopefully having understood how to go about designing the church's infrastructure, we can move to the development of a culturally oriented strategy.

Chapter Sixteen

Eighth Component of an Effective Ministry Plan: A CULTURALLY ORIENTED STRATEGY

T he pieces of the ministry plan puzzle finally start coming together when a culturally oriented strategy is put in place. This is the phase in which the ministry plan becomes most individualized and targeted for a particular environment. The specific people and local culture you are attempting to affect with the gospel will determine the means through which the message is communicated.

In case I haven't made it clear yet, my passion in ministry has a lot to do with discipleship. That priority remains unchanged no matter where I find myself. What have changed are the cultural factors that have influenced the way I practice discipleship. For example, I discovered the hard way that the almost unlimited opportunities to organize and practice discipleship I experienced in college were severely limited by the pressures and time constraints of life in the adult world. I had to rethink my methods of discipleship so that my passion would not become frustrated.

But cultural orientation is not an easy task. Anticipate learning through mistakes and failures. Keep in mind that God is sovereign over culture. Watch for ways in which God has already infiltrated the culture you are trying to reach. He has a way of building in unique features in each culture that provide a point of vulnerability to what He wants to accomplish. Maintain flexibility in methodology even as you are inflexible about the content of the gospel and God's Word.

Remember that to *determine your mission* you answer the question, "How will we accomplish our *vision?*" Your *strategy* is decided by continually asking the question, "How will we accomplish our *mission?*" Each question will push you to deal with particular issues that must be resolved in order to accomplish your vision.

Be mindful that moving through each step in the development of a ministry plan can be applied to the church as a whole, and then to every specific ministry within the whole (for example, music ministry or youth ministry). This is where *alignment* has a crucial role. *Every individual ministry plan must be in alignment with the overall ministry plan.*

Regardless of the uniqueness of a church's ministry plan, four universal questions must be answered in the development of a culturally oriented strategy. They are the following:

1. In what ways and to what degree will the unchurched be reached and hurting people be helped?
2. In what ways and to what degree will new people be folded into the family of God?
3. In what ways and to what degree will God's people learn biblical truth?
4. In what ways and to what degree will people be shepherded?

After addressing these four questions, I will address the specific issues of an individual church, using Perimeter Church's strategy as an example.

IN WHAT WAYS AND TO WHAT DEGREE WILL THE UNCHURCHED BE REACHED AND HURTING PEOPLE BE HELPED?

There's a familiar saying, "There are many ways to skin the cat!" Well, the same applies to reaching the unchurched. Any one, or better yet, many or all of the following approaches are options that can be used. The choice becomes, which one or ones will the church embrace? And if multiple approaches, which one gets the greater investment of resources? These are four of the most effective options.

Worship Services

The big question facing churches since the emergence of Willow Creek and the seeker service in the late 1970s has become, "Will we be a seeker church?"

It is common to have a potential church planter call me to talk about starting a new church. I typically ask him to describe the church he plans to plant. Quite often I hear, "It's going to be a Willow Creek type of church." I assume by this response that the person is referring to a church that will use the weekend services to reach the unchurched and will gather believers during the midweek for worship.

Because of my good friendship with Willow Creek's pastor, Bill Hybels, and because I have a high respect and appreciation for that church, I respond positively—yet with a well-worn follow-up question: "What are the downsides to such a strategy?" Unfortunately, the usual response is a blank stare and the admission that he has not considered any downsides. The point, of course, is that every strategy has its downside. By choosing one specific road, you have also chosen many roads you will not travel. Every action you decide to take involves a number of actions you have decided not to take.

In a later chapter, I will specifically address the issue of hard decisions on continuum issues. But as we deal with the continuum issue of *seeker* versus *believer* in the strategy used for weekend services, let me say now what will be explained later: Continuum choices (such as between traditional and contemporary; seeker and believer focuses) usually create contrasting weaknesses.

I typically ask the following questions of the pastor enamored with the seeker service model:

- *When will believers worship?*
- *When will you do small groups?*
- *When will you train leaders?*
- *When will Christians get educated?*
- *When do believers worship who travel during the week?*
- *How many times can a typical family be involved in church activities and still be functionally stable?*

The pie of time is only so big. You can cut it up many different ways, but every slice devoted to one value takes away time from another important value. The adage often rings true, "If it's too good to be true, it's too good to be true." No strategy choice is without downsides. The culture, particular demographic of people being reached, and the gift mix of church leadership all are important factors in deciding which strategy to use.

I am not trying to argue here against a seeker service but am trying to suggest that churches and church planters should count the cost carefully before using such a strategy. I think those who claim to hold to the high values of worship and equipping the saints must be relatively certain that their strategy actually allows those values to be experienced in the church. The strategy must also be effective in a way that fits today's modern culture. Also, as I said in an earlier chapter, pastors and laymen ought not to lobby for midweek worship if their theology (right or wrong) leaves them with the conviction that believers should worship on the Lord's Day. Never allow pragmatic zeal (even for such a lofty value as reaching the lost) to be motivation for theological compromise.

Even if you choose not to go the seeker service route, sound biblical worship can take place in such a way as to reach the nonbeliever. Simply by being sensitive to the nonbelievers' presence, carefully choosing language that relates to the unchurched, and by creatively applying the preaching of God's Word to the lost as well as to believers, the worship service can become a place for many to meet Christ. Observing authentic worship can be stimulating to the lost, causing them to want to continue attending. It is then that God often uses the constant exposure to His Word and His people to bring His chosen into His fold.

Small Groups

There is no better environment for equipping and accountability than a small group. Thus, such groups become excellent vehicles to win the lost. Groups could be evangelistic (inviting the unchurched to attend), or they could be equipping stations to launch individual believers into the mission fields in which they live, work, and play.

I mentioned in chapter 10 how Korea's Yoido Full Gospel Church's use of small groups to win the lost demonstrates how effective small groups can be as vehicles for outreach. Their commitment to win the lost is such that discipline is expected for failure to be fruitful. I'm not suggesting church discipline for failure to reach the lost, but Central Church's practice does illustrate that in certain cultures small groups can be used effectively to reach the lost.

Specialty Programs

Addressing the crisis needs of people in common struggle has proven to be an effective way of reaching nonbelievers. Whether it be alcohol and drug addiction, AIDS, cancer, crisis pregnancy, the death of a loved one, or divorce, programs designed to help people in their times of hardship are great opportunities to introduce them to Christ.

One nationally recognized program designed by one of our staff members, Bob Burns, called "Fresh Start," has been a tremendous tool for reaching the lost. People who have experienced the pain of separation and divorce are invited to this weekend seminar. Following the seminar, they are invited to continue meeting weekly with a support group of people in common crisis known as "Genesis." The program is nothing more than the application of the saying, "Find a need and fill it." But as the need is being addressed, the One who alone can and will meet their deepest needs is introduced. Such specialty programs are valuable tools for reaching the lost.

Individual Equipping

Chapters 20 and 21 will deal in more detail about the preparation of individual believers for the work of ministry. Suffice it to say that believers need to experience two significant areas of training if they are going to be effective ministers to others:

1. They must see their pastors and leaders practicing the disciplines of the spiritual life, particularly the sharing of their faith with others on a personal basis. This is training by modeling.
2. They must be equipped, encouraged, and expected to share their faith with others as one of the primary expressions of their growth in discipleship.

These two areas must be addressed in conscious ways if a church is serious about prevailing.

Community Bridge Building

Though touched on under "Specialty Programs," more needs to be said about meeting needs where people live. Nearly two years previous to celebrating our twenty-fifth anniversary as a church, we began to labor intensively seeking to determine what adjustments in ministry needed to be made as we launch our ministry into its second quarter of a century.

Our elders urged me to come with whatever recommendations for change I thought necessary, regardless of how radical they might be. As I shared my ideas, most of which related to "giving ourselves away for the sake of the least and the lost," one of our staff members handed me a book written by a good friend of mine. With the handing of the book, our staff member said, "You've got to read this book. It's just what you are talking about." That book was *The Church of Irresistible Influence*, by Robert Lewis.[1]

AN ASSIMILATION STRATEGY SHOULDN'T NECESSARILY BE EQUATED WITH MERELY GETTING PEOPLE INTO MEMBERSHIP

I will say nothing more at this point than to urge every person to read this book. Robert says with clarity and experience what every church, including ours, needs to learn. This book, plus Tim Keller's book *Ministries of Mercy*,[2] are helping to shape our church's future strategy to build bridges from our church into the communities in which we live, work and play—all with the intention of allowing our deeds to speak to people's needs as loudly as our words.

So, the first question that must be answered in forming a culturally oriented strategy is, "In what ways and to what degree will the unchurched be reached and hurting people be helped?" Regardless of the strategy chosen, just make sure that reaching the unchurched remains a priority.

IN WHAT WAYS AND TO WHAT DEGREE WILL NEW PEOPLE BE FOLDED INTO THE FAMILY OF GOD?

Perhaps more important than the choice of strategy is the very existence of a strategy everyone can understand and have confidence in. An assimilation strategy shouldn't necessarily be equated with merely getting people into membership. Assimilation can be achieved both by getting attenders relationally connected to others in the church and by giving attenders ownership of the ministry where they feel they can make a valuable contribution. Both these endeavors can be challenging tasks.

In part because of the fast-paced society in which we live today, deep relationships are hard to come by. There seems to be the mentality in churches today that it is the church's responsibility to give its people relationships. Not so. It is the believer's own responsibility to build personal relationships. It is not uncommon today for an insecure spouse to feel unloved by a very loving and adoring mate. Yet past relational experiences have conditioned them to believe they are unlovable. Thus, regardless of the love demonstrated, it cannot be received. Likewise, among those entering churches, opportunities for meeting people do not guarantee deep relationships. In addition to the problems created by individual insecurities, the modern fast pace of life makes relationship building difficult. Chuck Swindoll famously said, "Busyness rapes relationships" (*Killing Giants, Pulling Thorns*). And it is so true. Regardless of how you cut it, a large investment of time is required to produce meaningful relationships.

All this to say: Church leaders should not beat themselves up when newcomers find it hard to make relationships. Yet it is wise to develop a strategy that makes it as easy as possible to get connected relationally.

Groups of different sizes provide a variety of relational options. As mentioned in the previous chapter, the larger the group, the more opportunity the group provides socially because there are more options for people to meet and connect. The smaller the group, the deeper the relationship can go due to vulnerable sharing and caring for one another. But any way you look at it, small- to medium-sized groups (five to fifty) are great forums to help establish relationships.

Another rule of thumb to follow is that new people assimilate best with new people. After a while, people in a group fill their relational cups (especially those in a season of life with multiple young children). Group members may have good intentions about reaching out to newcomers, yet long-term groups tend to display what might be called "institutional neglect." Smiles and handshakes may be abundant, but little to no room is left over for new relationships. So, try as hard as they may, it is typically difficult for people to break in to longtime existing groups. A wise strategy is to continually form new groups.

In addition to offering a variety of *sizes* of groups, it also helps in assimilation to offer a variety in the *types* of groups. We have found that if we provide three types of small groups everyone can find a group that fits with his or her needs and/or wants. We offer fellowship, service, and equipping groups. Each type of group majors in that which its name implies and minors in the other two functions. For instance, a service group majors in serving and minors in fellowship and growth.

Our fellowship groups vary in size and activities. They are not high-commitment groups, but offer informal entry points to congregational life. They function much as Sunday school classes function in many churches. Their names give some clue to their identity: Neighborhood Congregations, Seasons of Life Communities, and Home Fellowships. These groups are not designed as ends but as beginning places for participation in the whole life of the church.

Our service groups are divided into three types: (1) those that serve during the weekend services; (2) those that provide ministries within our church; and (3) those which serve people who have needs within the communities in which we live, work, and play. Each group has a shepherd to offer care to all the group members.

Among our equipping groups, the most important are what we call Discipleship Teams. Each Discipleship Team has a leader who goes through weekly training on Sunday mornings and is under the leadership and care of a coach. Each coach is under the leadership and care of a staff pastor.

All three types of groups are important. God calls us to different places in various seasons of our lives. Such a variety of offerings assures an opportunity for each individual to find his or her best fit.

As I have already mentioned, having a sense of contributing to the mission of the church is a good way to get assimilated. Making it easy to find a task (especially one which employs one's spiritual gifts, talents, and interests) lessens the difficulty of getting assimilated. Working side by side with fellow believers in ministry is an excellent way to make lasting friendships.

Connecting Points

To help our people get assimilated, we introduce them to what we call "connecting points." These points highlight the primary means by which most of our people will establish relationships and find an opportunity to make a contribution to the mission of the church.

The connecting points include six important components:

1. Attending weekend worship services
2. Joining the church
3. Serving in a ministry
4. Joining a small group
5. Taking Perimeter's membership equipping courses (to be explained later)
6. Taking Perimeter's leadership training courses (and assuming ministry leadership along with ongoing training)

This list captures the intentionality and the progression of assimilation in our strategy.

IN WHAT WAYS AND TO WHAT DEGREE WILL GOD'S PEOPLE LEARN BIBLICAL TRUTH?

Several years ago, we invited Roberta Hestenes, then president of Eastern College, to do a seminar at our church on small groups. One of the comments she made which I'll never forget was that she feared the impact of the modern church growth movement on the church of future generations. Her question: "With the popular models for church today, when and where will people learn the Bible? Where will people learn the book of Isaiah?" What a challenge!

There are numerous ways to answer these concerns. The four I've included represent what we consider our most strategic responses to this pressing need.

The Pulpit

Many pastors, especially those coming out of a Reformed tradition in theology, bank almost solely on the pulpit for educating their people. The strength of this tradition is the high view of the Scriptures and the dependence upon the work of the Holy Spirit. Yet as we have seen earlier, Scripture places much emphasis on the additional value of truth being conveyed in a relational context (what I call *life-on-life*).

Even while we embrace a high view of preaching, we must also admit that the preaching of God's Word can be either effective or ineffective. Both *what* is said and *how* it is said play significant roles in determining effectiveness.

After affirming that the truth of God's Word is to be the substance of one's preaching, the next priority is to determine one's goal for preaching. Is the goal primarily to educate God's people? Or is the goal to challenge God's people? Or is it both, or even something else? Is it directed to seekers, young believers, or mature believers?

I am convinced that the goal of preaching should be to bring God's Word to bear upon people in every stage of spiritual pilgrimage in such a way as to bring every person under the lordship of Christ in every area of life.

I believe that for approximately the first ten years of my ministry I had an improper understanding of the purpose of my preaching. My shift in understanding is perhaps best captured in one of my journal notes in July of 1990:

> To aim at a Bible passage as one preaches, periodically making applications to personal life, will leave the believing community convinced they have been taught by God's man. But to aim at a personal life while preaching, bringing God's truth to bear upon its need, will leave the believing community convinced they have been taught by God's Spirit.

My understanding of preaching was much impacted by the teaching of Haddon Robinson, who wrote:

> Life changing preaching does not talk to people about the Bible. Instead, it talks to people about themselves (their questions, lusts, fears and struggles) from the Bible. The basic principle in preaching is to give as much biblical information as the people need to understand the passage, and no more. Then move on to your application. When we approach the sermon with that philosophy, flint strikes steel. The flint of someone's problems strikes the steel of the Word of God, and a spark ignites that can set that person on fire for God.[3]

I am discouraged to see how often intellectual stimulation is more desired than spiritual vitalization. Though preaching must certainly be intellectually challenging, that can never be the goal in sight.

Especially since the early 1970s, there has been much debate concerning the appropriate approach to preaching. When I began pastoral ministry, those I admired the most championed expositional teaching through books of the Bible as the "most biblical approach." Topical preaching was viewed as significantly inferior, if even acceptable at all. The lack of compelling reasons for such a conclusion, in addition to examples of great preachers of the past, such as Charles Spurgeon, who didn't always preach through books of the Bible, left me with skepticism.

When I attended seminary, in addition to approximately one-third of our time spent studying practical theology, about one-third of the curriculum was given to biblical theology (learning the text verse by verse). The other one-third of our curriculum concentrated on systematic theology (studying the topics of God's Word by drawing upon texts throughout the Bible). It appeared to me then, as it does to me these years later, that expository preaching is nothing more than preaching that concentrates on biblical theology, whereas topical preaching focuses on systematic theology. It seems to me that each is equally valuable to sound preaching. They reinforce each other.

There is a third category of preaching that is a blend of the two—

perhaps we could call it topical exposition. An illustration of this would be preaching on a topic such as celibacy but doing so simply by expositing what Paul had to say to the people of Corinth in his first epistle.

Perhaps some preachers would decide that they can best steward their teaching or exhortation gifts by primarily doing one of the preaching approaches. I personally enjoy them all, finding my typical year's preaching calendar divided, giving approximately 25 percent to expository preaching, 25 percent to topical teaching, and 50 percent to topical exposition.

I would suggest that every church make sure that there is balance in the full offerings of the church. If the pastor primarily teaches using expository preaching, make sure that topical study of the Word is offered elsewhere in the life of the church.

Church members often get disgruntled at the approach their pastor uses when he preaches. They remember well how they grew so quickly as a new Christian under a particular approach and now assume that their lack of continued spiritual growth is due to their pastor's using a different approach.

SMALL GROUPS CAN BE EXCELLENT VEHICLES FOR CHRISTIAN EDUCATION

Let me illustrate the absurdity of such a conclusion. I am of average height, and so are my wife and both of our families. It appeared throughout his childhood as though Matt, our first child, would be the same. However, when he was fifteen, he experienced an unusual growth spurt and ended up being six foot three inches (extremely tall for a Pope). During the next couple of years, people constantly asked him, "How'd you get so tall, boy?" If he answered accurately, his response would have been, "Eating pizza." That seemed to be all he wanted at that age (and I'm sure we gave in far too often). Matt could have easily concluded that if everyone else ate primarily pizza at age fifteen they too would grow tall.

Well, we know better. The truth is that we are all genetically wired to grow to a certain height. Only malnutrition will significantly alter our genetic wiring. The reality is that regardless of what Matt ate, as long as he was getting an adequate intake of nutrients, he was destined to grow to his genetically coded height.

So, too, with the Word of God. The Word causes us to grow regardless of how it is served. Most hearers have their preferred styles, but this does not invalidate other styles.

Having argued for the importance of preaching, I would suggest that preaching is not enough in and of itself to provide sufficient education for God's people. Let's look at some other forums for teaching the full counsel of God.

The Classroom

There are many different uses of the classroom in training believers, but perhaps the most familiar is Sunday school. Every exposure to God's Word is valuable, but most would agree that adult Sunday school is less than ideal for education. Many people are primarily motivated to attend for relational reasons. Few are willing to do outside study in preparation for their class. Add to this that a typical class has a widely varying attendance from week to week and a diverse audience spiritually (eager infant Christians, long-term believers with little appetite for growth, and extremely mature followers). Given these conditions, quality education is difficult at best. These reasons also explain why so many people who have attended adult Sunday schools for a lifetime are nevertheless biblically illiterate.

Elective courses designed with homework assignments are often better vehicles to help people gain biblical information. Whether in week-to-week or concentrated seminar fashion, the classroom can play a valuable role in the Christian's biblical education.

Small Groups

If one evaluates education based on what is learned rather than by what is taught, small groups will be viewed as an ideal forum for education. Perhaps this would be accepted as the norm if we had an abundance of able and willing instructors. Few, if any, churches have enough knowledgeable, gifted communicators to supply large numbers of small groups with teachers. But modern technology has alleviated some of the constraints created when education depends on the teacher alone to deliver the truth. By using study books, tapes, and well-written curriculum, good education can take place in small groups of any sized church. As will be discussed in depth in a later chapter, the small size of such groups allows for equipping and accountability, which are important components of life-altering education.

Whether studying books of the Bible or topics related to Christian living or theology, small groups can be excellent vehicles for Christian education.

Personal Study

In my opinion, by far the best way to learn biblical truth is through personal study. Such learning can take place through daily personal worship as well as through regular personal Bible study. I have often said that I have learned more at the Bedside School of the Bible than I ever learned in all the seminars, Sunday school classes, Bible conferences, and seminary classes I attended combined.

Much like learning to do evangelism well, believers need to learn one primary approach or method for partaking of Christ's truth that best serves them. Such personal worship and study methods need to be included in the equipping provided in the church's discipleship ministry.

These are just four of many different venues for learning biblical truth. Developing a culturally relevant strategy will require you to determine to what extent you will use these or other means.

IN WHAT WAYS AND TO WHAT DEGREE
WILL PEOPLE BE SHEPHERDED?

Ask pastors what their approach to shepherding is and you will often hear them describe a new approach they are initiating to replace a plan that has not worked well. Candidly, shepherding the flock is more like keeping up with cats than sheep. They often move quickly, can be very evasive, and are sometimes so temperamental they don't want to be petted.

But God leaves no room for dismissal of this task. Peter, speaking under inspiration of God, says to elders, "Shepherd the flock of God among you, exercising oversight not under compulsion, but voluntarily, according to the will of God; and not for sordid gain, but with eagerness; nor yet as lording it over those allotted to your charge, but proving to be examples to the flock" (1 Peter 5:2–3).

In the Book of Hebrews, God speaks soberly to us when the author, addressing believers, says, "Obey your leaders and submit to them, for they keep watch over your souls as those who will give an account" (Hebrews 13:17).

So how does a church do a good job of keeping up with its people so as to care for them well? Like most endeavors that are successful, there needs to be a plan to accomplish the task. Such workable plans can be constructed around geography, seasons of life, small groups, and other grouping categories. The important thing is that the span of care is reasonable in size; the leadership responsible for shepherding is qualified, well-trained, and faithful to the task; and that those in shepherding positions are cared for themselves. It is certainly ideal to align one's shepherding strategy as closely as possible to discipleship (as discipleship is indeed the purest form of shepherding). But realistically, many within the church family will not be in discipleship groups.

Because each church and culture (racial, economic, and geographical) is so different, I will not suggest one grouping category to be superior over the others. However, I do believe that every individual in the church who desires to be shepherded should have a specific designated leader responsible to that task. Members should be responsible to participate in the worship and work of the church. Their unwillingness to do so should rightly cause them to forfeit the more mature levels of care and shepherding that people need. Those responsibilities and privileges should be carefully spelled out for those in membership. (Our church uses the membership questions written by the Westminster Divines in the 1600s that include a promise "to participate in the worship and work of the church.")

We now structure our ministry in such a way that all people could be in some form of small group unless providentially hindered by health or unique circumstances (and then special care must be offered). Whether in a fellowship, service, or equipping group, someone is designated as a leader of the group and carries the responsibility of being a shepherd to those who participate. This means that every volunteer in our church should be cared for by a leader.

It is of utmost importance that each leader is cared for by a shepherd (some call those coaching shepherds), and if the organization is large enough, those coaching shepherds must be shepherded by a pastor (usually a staff member or a lay pastor).

Shepherding goals are critical measuring rods to determine how non-crisis care is being accomplished. Those goals could include the following:

- Implementing the church's "who we are" values (for example, love, integrity, faith, and truth)
- Evaluating those being discipled by using the description of a mature and equipped follower of Christ (for example, "Live under the direction of the Word of God, the control of the Holy Spirit, and the compelling love of Christ")
- Meeting the participation goals set by the church (for example, consistent worship, church membership, and small-group participation)

Corrective Shepherding

Corrective shepherding is ultimately only as good as the willingness of the church leadership to discipline erring members. God has given the "keys to the kingdom to elders" to be used when needed. Those keys must sometimes be used to unlock membership doors, so as to allow unrepentant members to be dismissed from membership ("Let him be unto thee as an heathen man," Matthew 18:17 KJV). I am grieved to see how few churches, otherwise known to be great churches, are unwilling to exercise this means of grace to those who are in need of it.

Though biblical shepherding may be difficult, it is absolutely imperative—from noncrisis loving care and concern, to crisis care, to restorative church discipline. Would that the church once again claim its full responsibilities in this endeavor.

Specific Strategy

Once the four broad questions are answered, there also remains the task of dealing specifically with the individual strategy issues related to the church's specific mission (remember, strategy is determined by answering the question, "How will we go about accomplishing our mission?").

For Perimeter Church that means answering these questions:

1. How will we go about making mature and equipped followers of Christ?
2. What will we do to become a church of compassion comprised of praying people willing to give ourselves away for the cause of the least and the lost?
3. How will we build strategic bridges between our church and the communities in which we live, work, and play?
4. How will we plant new churches and partner with existing churches across Atlanta and around the world to strategically do the above?

You can see in reading this list that these questions force us to align every aspect of our ministry. We previously went into great detail on the first of these four. I regret not addressing these last three as specifically. My intention here, however, is to merely use them as a model to illustrate how one goes about designing a culturally relevant strategy that accomplishes the church's mission.

With the strategy determined, the hard work is over. Now all that's left is establishing goals and determining an appropriate schedule to follow.

NOTES

1. Robert Lewis (with Rob Wilkins) *The Church of Irresistible Influence* (Grand Rapids: Zondervan, 2001).

2. Timothy J. Keller, *Ministries of Mercy: The Call of the Jericho Road* (Phillipsburg: P & R, 1997).

3. Haddon Robinson, quoted in *Making a Difference in Preaching*, by Scott Gibson (Grand Rapids: Baker, 1990), 94.

———⊶⊷———

Chapter Seventeen

Ninth Component of an Effective Ministry Plan: WELL-DOCUMENTED GOALS

P erhaps of all the components that make up a ministry plan, goal setting is the one most in dispute. Many faithful followers of Christ have argued that goals are inappropriate tools. "Goals," they have said, "presume upon God and seek to make man's ways, God's ways. Goals attempt to control and perhaps quench the Holy Spirit. Goals limit God."

To the contrary, it would be fairer to say that a lack of goals actually limits God's work more than goal setting. Even the simplest goals get a life or a group in motion. Lack of goals leaves a life's and a group's transmission in Park. Even if goals are not appropriate, they serve in such a way to validate the saying, "It's easier to steer a vehicle in motion than it is to steer a parked car."

The concept of goals is certainly not foreign to the Scriptures. Jesus Himself, in response to warnings of danger from Herod, said "Go tell that fox, 'Behold, I cast out demons and perform cures today and tomorrow, and the third day I reach My goal'" (Luke 13:32 NASB). The Apostle Paul refers to man's ultimate goal in Philippians 3:14, "I press on toward the goal for the prize of the upward call of God in Christ Jesus" (NASB).

Paul's blend of moving toward a goal yet being submissive to whatever the Lord might have in store for him appears at the close of 1 Corinthians. Paul wrote, "I will come to you after I go through Macedonia, for I am going through Macedonia. . . . For I do not wish to see you now just in passing; for I hope to remain with you for some time, *if the Lord permits.* But I will remain in Ephesus until Pentecost" (1 Corinthians 16:3–8, italics added).

Even a well-known passage such as James 4:13–17 NIV, which is sometimes quoted to discourage goal setting, actually encourages it. The passage starts out with what appears to be a devastating attack on goal setting:

Now listen, you who say, "Today or tomorrow we will go to this or that city, spend a year there, carry on business and make money." Why, you do not even know what will happen tomorrow. What is your life? You are a mist that appears for a little while and then vanishes.

But in the end, even while reproving any tendency to disregard God's will in goal setting—"You ought to say, 'If it is the Lord's will'"—it acknowledges the need for plans and goals: "We will live *and do this or that*" (v. 15, italics added).

"WHAT ARE THE NEXT STEPS GOD WANTS US TO TAKE IN THE PROCESS?"

Goal setting enables us to put expression and direction to an act of faith. Goals are simply targets. They are not to be viewed as dictates from

God. They can be changed and even missed without shame. We never forget that our goals set us in motion, but we fully expect God to steer the vehicle.

Goals help set the stage for action. As the authors of *Built to Last* have written, they are critical for "stimulating progress . . . [and] protecting a company's core ideology and the type of progress it aims to achieve."[1] They enable us to have a better sense of direction and purpose while allowing us to evaluate our progress. They help us to plan ahead and communicate within the organization. Without goals, those involved in the mission don't have a clear understanding of what is expected.

HOW WILL WE KNOW IF WE ARE ACCOMPLISHING OUR VISION AND MISSION?

Goals will ultimately be decided by answering the question, "How will we know if we are making progress toward accomplishing our vision and mission?" Goals represent the mile markers and signposts that tell us how we are doing. Using the familiar acronym SMART to describe goals is a good way to make sure that the goals being set are helpful. They must be *Specific, Measurable, Attainable, Realistic,* and *Time Bound.*

Specific

In chapter 3 we looked at seven factors that always have an impact on the growth of a local church. The fifth factor we listed as *adequate property, facilities,* and *parking.* Let's use these for examples of goal setting. Once you have decided what those requirements will mean in your setting, you will need to set down the incremental steps that will take you from your present situation to a plan the leadership will agree is adequate for your vision and mission. "A big building and lots of parking" is not a good example of specific goals.

Setting goals in this area will force the leadership of the church to demonstrate how clearly they understand and endorse the ministry plan. A good test of alignment is how often the mission and vision are quoted as the elders are discussing whether to add another worship service, for example. Aim at being specific and you will tend to hit clarity.

Measurable

Goals are a lot like budgets. In fact, establishing a budget represents one of the clearest examples of goal setting. That's probably why those who resist goal setting often resist establishing budgets. Motives, assumptions, and expectations all become clearer as we discuss the measurability of our goals. For instance, the vision of PMI is to achieve its goal of establishing one hundred congregations in the greater Atlanta area in the next ten years. It is important that the vision be broken down into yearly increments, with appropriate adjustments being made along the way.

Attainable

Healthy goal setting includes a conscious effort to express a vision in doable steps. The vision, by definition, has the appearance of implausibility and the characteristic, hopefully, of being so big that it is "doomed to failure unless God be in it." Without ever forgetting for a moment that God ultimately makes it happen, we must still answer the question, "What are the next steps God wants us to take in the process?" A goal needs to include specific action we can actually take.

Realistic

Realists often come across as pessimists. Most elder boards include at least one realist. A board made up exclusively of either idealists or realists is a frightening creature, but a healthy mix makes for good goal setting. Realists keep the steps from being too big. Many goals could be described as attainable that may not be realistic. One hundred percent of the congregation's members tithing may be attainable as a goal in the sense that they all could tithe, but not realistic if the present reality is 10 percent of the members of the church tithe. But increasing the current number of tithers to 20 percent would make a measurable impact on many aspects of church life.

Time Bound

Time factors are such an important aspect of a ministry plan that we will discuss them in greater detail in the next chapter. Motion, growth, and progress are almost always measured in both space and time. Healthy spiritual goals will include a consideration of time. There is a huge difference between my saying, "I'm going to share my faith in Christ with someone else sometime during my lifetime" and my saying, "I'm going to share my faith in Christ with someone this week." The first example is a very poor excuse for a goal and close to an expression of disobedience; the second puts me into the thick of God's work in the world.

Other Factors in Goal Setting

In addition to being SMART, goals must be supported by a plan, owned by those required to accomplish them, and supported by the necessary resources.

Most agree that goals should be determined for both the short term and the long term. There seems to be a consensus that short-term goals should be annual and that long-term goals typically cover a three- to five-year span, with a recent movement toward the shorter side of that span.

A full discussion of goal setting is simply not possible in this book, but there are some excellent resources available for further study. One that I have appreciated is James Collins and Jerry Porras' book *Built to Last*, from which I have already quoted. They have a great chapter about the importance of BHAGs (Big Hairy Audacious Goals). They claim that every organization needs at least one or two goals that are set big enough and even outrageous enough to create a sense of vision and enthusiasm in the hearts of those responsible to accomplish the task.

Such goals certainly inspire people, but for believers it is important to make sure that the motive for goal setting is that of meeting needs, not merely accomplishing astonishing results. Likewise, it is very important when setting goals not to allow them to be based upon the past or upon personal preferences. The leading of God must be the reason for choosing the goals that are set. Having said that, a healthy application of the BHAG principle brings to the goal-setting process the same kind of stretch and faith that characterizes our definition of a worthy vision— an effort of such magnitude that it is bound to fail unless God is in it.

Another helpful resource is the book *Encouraging the Heart*, by James Kouzes and Barry Posner. They note that feedback when setting and monitoring goals is critical if we expect to see them met. In their work, they refer to a Stanford University study showing that goals alone result in about a 24 percent improvement in performance effort. When feedback is added, there is a staggering 59 percent improvement.[2] This is simply a statistical confirmation of the power of accountability. Staff reviews that measure current performance against previously agreed upon goals is a fair approach to doing evaluations. Such use of goals is especially beneficial when feedback, encouragement, and development are the focus.

WHO SETS THE GOALS?

Perhaps the last issue to be addressed is, "Who sets the goals?" Though there is not an agreed-upon answer by all, I believe there is wisdom in allowing the pastor to start the goal-setting process. Time spent in prayer and seeking the mind of God should be the starting point. In a multiple-staffed church, other staff members should share their counsel (and have major influence in the goals that relate to their specific ministry). In an elder-led church, the elders should have final approval. As the senior pastor, my evaluation is determined in part by my performance against the goals. Thus, it is important that we agree on the goals that are ultimately used.

NEXT

Once you have completed your strategy, begin setting goals. Then use those goals as a primary focus of prayer. Once goals are in place, all that's left is setting your ministry plan to a schedule.

NOTES

1. James C. Collins and Jerry I. Porras, *Built to Last* (New York: HarperCollins, 1994, 1997), 93, 202.
2. James M. Kouzes and Barry Z. Posner, *Encouraging the Heart: A Leader's Guide to Rewarding and Recognizing Others* (San Francisco: Jossey-Bass, 1998).

—⊶⊷⊶—

Chapter Eighteen

Tenth Component of an Effective Ministry Plan: A TIME-BOUND SCHEDULE

A s important as timing is to the punch line of a comedian, so too is timing critical to instigating new endeavors or, more important, instigating change. When an idea we originally thought was good turns out to be a miserable mistake, we often conclude that the idea was wrong or bad. In reality, the idea may have been excellent but was implemented too early or too late. Or perhaps the problem wasn't timing itself but just plain hurry. We may have tried to implement the idea before it was understood and bought by those for whom it was intended.

The last chapter included a discussion of the acrostic SMART that represents the qualities required for good goal setting. The *T* stands for *time bound*. We argued that a built-in time factor is part of an effective goal. Otherwise, a specific, measurable, attainable, and realistic goal languishes for lack of a time-oriented accountability. Almost every other point of accountability becomes useless without a time factor.

In order to develop a time-bound schedule, we must answer the question, "What is a reasonable time line of specific tasks that must take place in order to accomplish the goals of our ministry plan?" Here is often where we discover if our goals are truly reasonable. How many times have we missed our goals not because we had unreasonable goals or did the wrong things, but simply because we did the right things in the wrong sequence? Establishing a schedule is an invaluable tool. The final determination whether our goals are really SMART comes when we place them together in a schedule. Sometimes, individual goals must have their measurable, attainable, and realistic factors altered in order to fit in a time-specific structure with other goals.

Decisions about when to do certain things require great wisdom. The merits of an idea alone are not enough to establish a time line for implementation. In other words, deciding whether an idea is good and desirable is different from deciding if and when it should be accepted and implemented.

CHANGE AND TIME

People resist change. Their resistance rarely flows from a thoughtful rejection of the proposed change itself. More often than not, people resist change because they simply don't like change. So it serves us well to know something about change management. Many of my acquaintances are laughing right now as they think about the idea of my writing on this subject. I readily admit that yesterday is too late for me regarding any desired change. I also admit that it is healthy, challenging, and maddeningly frustrating for me to help lead an organization that by nature resists change. The process develops patience in me, though I do find myself uttering that classic prayer, "Lord, make me patient . . . now!"

It is important that we don't merely set goals for the sake of change, but that we carefully think through what changes we need to achieve.

Once those issues are clear, we can then discuss how best to manage that change with a large number of people. Such input may well have us change our time line and sometimes the goals themselves. Better not to try a change unless we can be reasonably sure that the changes will be embraced by our people.

You may remember that I mentioned in the Introduction that some of the material in this book will have undergone change by the time you read it, but I was simply trying to practice what I preach. People will appreciate the truth and timelessness of the core of faith if they are continually reminded that the external (and sometimes useful) trappings are subject to change.

Certainly there are times when the best change management is to simply make the change without flagging it. I have far too often invited resistance by seeking to get ownership from our people when, in reality, few if any would have even noticed the change.

Because change comes so hard for so many, it is often best, when possible, to merely add new initiatives without killing the old ones. The key words are *when possible*. Some new programs cannot exist alongside the old, and thus coexistence is not possible. But when it is possible, all the better.

I have been told that in the bayou, where buildings are built on stilts, the conditions cause rapid rotting of those stilts. Instead of replacing the old ones, however, new ones are merely added. As the old ones rot and the waters move in and out, the old stilts eventually wash away. Similarly, it is often the wisest choice to allow old programs to die natural deaths while the new ones thrive.

On the other hand, I'm not advocating change for the sake of change. I've spent a good deal of time thinking and journaling on this subject. Here are a couple of samples for your consideration:

I remain alarmed at the ever-increasing rise of consumerism in church. I have to deal with it nearly every day in some form or fashion. The lost world seeks for satisfaction by going from toy to toy, relationship to relationship, and fix to fix. We know that only Christ can fill that void. For the Christian, many are no different from the world. Their toys, fixes, and relationships are substituted for church programs, ministries, experiences, and new biblical teachings. But only Christ, yielding His glory deposited in our lives, can fully satisfy. As a pastor, I often feel I am pressured to keep manufacturing programs, ministries, and teachings that "fill their needs" in order to keep people satisfied; and I become weary of this. I often feel like a spouse must feel when, though being a good mate, still finds his or her spouse dissatisfied. I counsel such people not to beat themselves up, yet I tend to do the very same thing when people are not satisfied with my best efforts to give them what they need.

There are so many consumer paradoxes that have me baffled:

- People want something new, fresh, and exciting but do not want change.
- People want to go deep but don't want to invest the time to go there.
- People want deep, interesting, relevant, and well-illustrated messages but want them to be short and simple.
- People want more and more services provided but don't want to keep being asked to serve in the support of those services.
- People want to be communicated to better but don't want special meetings for the purpose of communications and get fed up with so much mail and e-mail coming to their homes.

And the list goes on and on.

When it comes to the leader deciding when to initiate changes, he must be discerning in measuring gains versus losses. Most people want change without losses, and such is so rare that leaders are often unwilling to initiate necessary changes. Yet when gains do outweigh losses, it's usually an indicator that it's time to pull the trigger for the good of the majority of those being led. God, make me wise in my discernment of gains and losses and secure enough in You to embrace the criticism that comes with leading change. Lord, thanks for the privilege to participate in leading change that results in Your glory. I love You.

PRIORITIES AND CHANGE

When we launched into our emphasis on discipleship, we knew we would have to make hard decisions. Some things, such as our Sunday morning adult communities, could not coexist with our leadership training groups because of lack of space. Thus they had to be discontinued. However, our Home Fellowship Communities (our former small-group ministry) were permitted to continue (some of which are still in existence now, several years later). Though we formed no new groups, those that wanted to continue did so. However, staff and other leadership attention was given to forming new types of groups that were in alignment with our newly embraced mission and vision. We will visit this subject again in the next chapter on hard decisions.

PULSE-TAKING AND CHANGE

In order to assess the impact of changes to be made, we find that focus groups serve us well. They enable us to hear from a representative sampling of our congregation regarding three areas:

❧ *What issues will we face when we introduce the change?*
❧ *What resistance will be offered as a result of the change?*
❧ *What needs and concerns have perhaps been overlooked?*

Sometimes the understanding or questions of someone who hasn't been part of the discussion reveal some startling assumptions that have been missed during the planning for change.

SCHEDULING BACKWARDS

I suggest developing schedules by starting at the date the goals are to be accomplished and working backward. As this process unfolds, you will see if reasonable time has been allotted and whether your goals can actually be accomplished. This process has helped us avoid a good deal of late and frustrating schedule changes caused by poor planning at the outset.

DONE—EXCEPT

With this last piece of the puzzle in place, your ministry plan will be complete. Now only one thing will be left—execution.

As you get started, let me warn you right now that though this adventure will be invigorating and the impact on your church will be enlarged, get ready for stress. You're in for some difficult choices.

Chapter Nineteen

———⚬⚭⚬———

Difficult Choices

Designing a ministry plan is a rigorous exercise in making difficult choices. That is probably the main reason so few people attempt to do it. That is also why I am convinced that a ministry plan is one of the most overlooked factors in determining the growth potential of a church. I've talked to pastors in countless churches that clearly exhibit six of the factors we described in chapter 3. What they lack is an effective ministry plan. And one reason they don't have a plan is that they consciously or unconsciously recoil from the difficult choices and dangerous waters they will have to navigate in order to develop such a plan. But I believe the voyage is completely worthwhile.

UPSIDE, DOWNSIDE

Through the years of leading our church, I have come to realize that choices, such as those mentioned in the earlier chapters, are difficult because most decisions create contrasting problems. Let me illustrate.

Most difficult choices are made on a continuum between contrasting values or priorities, and in most churches, there are fierce proponents of either extreme. Here are some of the continuums:

Seeker	Believer
Traditional	Contemporary
Single-minded focus	Variety and choice
Program oriented	Discipleship oriented
Top-down leadership	Bottom-up leadership
Spiritual growth emphasis	Social emphasis

We rarely have the option of making a decision that results only in advantages. I will illustrate using one of the continuums above: *Single-minded focus versus Variety and choice focus*.

When you think about effective evangelism, which parachurch organization comes immediately to mind? Most of us will agree—Campus Crusade for Christ. Why are they known for such effective evangelism? In large part because they are so singularly focused. Everyone in Crusade must use "The Four Spiritual Laws." No other method is sanctioned. Regarding personal methods, there is absolutely no option for variety. Regarding stylistic preferences, a staff member's choice is not considered. As a result, many people choose not to be involved with Crusade. Many are even critical of Crusade's narrowness (or perhaps, better said, its single-minded focus).

Campus Crusade has made a choice. They chose to be extremely strong in evangelism by being singularly focused regarding their method. At the same time, they chose not to regard the individual needs and desires of their constituency. They are confident enough in their track record that they don't hesitate to encourage those who insist on an individualistic style of evangelism to practice it freely on their own, outside of Campus Crusade.

Strengths and Weaknesses

To move one way or the other on any of these continuums is likely to create a strength; and every strength on every continuum creates its own matching weakness. The stronger the emphasis on contemporary expression, the weaker will be the appeal to those who expect and appreciate traditional expressions. A highly program-oriented organization may present a structure that fits everyone, but the quality of discipleship for the individual believer will tend to be weaker.

What makes many choices so difficult is that they don't have to be made between the good and the bad, but rather between the good and the best. The good can be the enemy of the best; and many people like the spiritual good more than the spiritual best. Churches often lose healthy morale and people if they don't offer the good, yet can lose out in the kingdom if they are not offering the best. And the church can rarely offer both at the same time. The church, therefore, will never reach its full potential without its people developing a passionate desire to seek the best, not merely the good.

Alignment

The term *alignment* is a favored word around Perimeter. Our staff director has made sure that every staff member constantly thinks in terms of alignment.

Putting *Built to Last*'s definition of alignment into a ministry context, we define alignment as making sure that "all the elements of the *ministry* work together in concert within the context of the *church's* core ideology and the type of progress it aims to achieve."[1]

Alignment is not simply deciding that something is merely not opposed to one's vision. It is determining that whatever is embraced within the ministry *supports and progresses* the vision. Thus, the question to ask is not, "Is this practice good?" but rather, "Is this practice the best for us, fitting consistently with our ideology and mission?" Another question to ask of anything being considered is, "Would this move us closer or further away from our mission and vision?"

We faced such hard questions when we had to decide whether our adult communities, which met on Sunday morning, would enhance or hinder our effort to become a TEAMS-based church. Our decision, until additional space could be built, was to reassign the space used for adult communities to leadership training for those pastoring and discipling. Not a very popular decision! But it was certainly a decision in alignment with our vision. And the limitations of time and space made the decision unavoidable. Later, in a new facility, we were able to offer the adult community option again, without compromising our primary commitment to equipping and discipleship.

On another occasion, as I've already mentioned, a couple of our elders submitted a proposal that our church sponsor a Boy Scout troop that would attract families from the community. There was no question that this would be a good thing to do, but the request was eventually declined because we believed it would detract from our student ministry, which was integral to accomplishing the church's mission and vision. Such decisions are akin to cursing motherhood and apple pie. However, it is better to be aligned than popular. The more a ministry plan is understood and accepted by the congregation, the easier it is to weather these difficult decisions. When there is no clear mission and vision, anything "good" is much harder to turn away.

The Alignment Process

In order to determine alignment, it is important to define the activity in question, including the purpose, vision, mission, goals, and resources required. Then apply the previously discussed questions: "Does this activity fit with our church ideology (vision and core values) and does it promote the achievement of our goals?" Considering all of this, it's time to make a decision—sometimes a hard one.

Add to all that's been said the reality that the modern church, specifically in America, is absorbed in consumerism. People tend to treat their personal choices as the highest authority in their lives. Submission is often rejected simply because it challenges our "right" to do what we want. This makes our choices as leaders of Christ's church even harder. People today think much more in terms of what they want than in terms of what they need, and the gap between the two is growing rapidly.

The Real Needs

If people were choosing a church based on what they truly need, they would be most attracted to a church which has a

- passion for God's glory
- solid biblical theology
- commitment to and training for disciple making
- commitment to and training for disciple training
- commitment to church discipline

However, people are usually attracted to a church which has

- enjoyable preaching
- inspiring music
- enjoyable and convenient programming

A good friend of mine who pastors one of the fastest-growing churches in America was quoted in a national Christian magazine describing the mentality of the people at the church he pastors. He said, "We could change our theology and no one would care, but if we changed our music we would split the church." This is a sad commentary on the condition of the modern church.

CONGREGATIONAL PARADIGMS

So, pastors and church leaders, perhaps the biggest continuum decision you must make has to do with your values regarding which of the following two targets you would choose if you had to choose one over the other.

The first target is pictured by the diagram below:

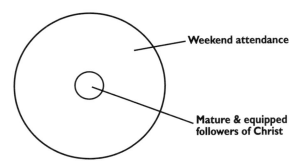

This diagram represents a church that is extremely popular among the community, possibly based on giving its people what they want, perhaps representing that which is good. This church often ends up functioning like Bud Wilkinson's famous description of a football crowd in a stadium on a weekend—"Twenty-two men on the field desperately needing rest, and fifty thousand people in the stands desperately needing exercise." (When Howard Hendricks tells this story, he concludes by saying, "What a description of the local church!") This model certainly fits a consumer-entertainment mentality. But does it please God?

The next diagram represents a second approach that focuses more on its people's needs (representing that which is best for the people).

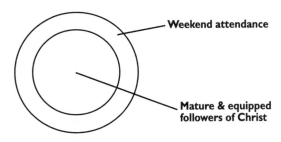

Note that the outer circle is not as large, yet the inner circle is considerably larger. This is not to say that the better the quality of the discipleship and ministry of a church, the lower the quantity of attendees and members. But it could possibly mean that.

Beginning with our first staff and officer retreats nearly twenty-five years ago, I have continuously kept these two targets before the leadership. I said then, and I'll say it now, there are decisions we can make that will make us a more enjoyable church yet less effective at making mature and equipped followers of Christ. My choice of targets lies clearly in the second. Ideally, we see the Lord give abundant fruit in growth (quantity) while making decisions based primarily on what will take our people through healthy spiritual formation (quality).

Tough Choices: Groups

When we decided to go to a discipleship-oriented ministry, the spiritual growth of a significant minority of our people accelerated measurably. However, in order to equip leaders to be effective disciple-trainers, we needed to give this training the best of our prime time and primary leadership. As I mentioned earlier, this meant that because we had limited space on Sunday morning, and limited leadership, we needed to discontinue adult Sunday school. This was a tough, unpopular choice. But we stuck by it because it was in clear alignment with our ministry plan. This decision enabled us to use our leaders and available rooms for equipping leaders who would be discipling and pastoring our people during the week. The results eventually demonstrated the wisdom of the choice.

In addition to this, we felt that we needed a more singular focus on discipleship and decided that for the first several years we would curtail other types of small groups that competed with discipleship teams for leadership and training resources.

The result was that, while the spiritual formation of our people excelled significantly, the sense of satisfaction among many of our people decreased. The prevalent feeling of many in the church over the next few years was that fellowship in the church had diminished and that life at Perimeter was not as enjoyable as it used to be.

Several years later, after discipleship was firmly rooted in our church, we were able to add other types of groups with the belief that these offerings could now serve as a funnel into discipleship (without threatening the health of our most valued nurturing ministry).

Tough Choices: Young People and Worship

Another example of a choice posing a challenge to church leadership has to do with the felt need of parents and their children and youth to have worship services designed specifically for the children and youth. Here the leadership members need to ask themselves, *What is the best for the young people?* (We certainly know what their wants are, but what about their needs?)

Depending on where you land on this issue, you may have a hard choice. You may believe that such accommodating worship services are unhealthy. You see them producing high school graduates who have never been to adult worship or seen their parents worship, and who will struggle with church throughout college and adulthood because the music and worship style are not their preference. (I recently heard a reputable speaker say that youth who attend youth worship rather than worship with adults are far more likely to drop out of church when they attend college. Though I don't know his source of information, I would expect such to be the case.) If this be so, we might make a hard and unpopular decision. Such may well produce a healthier ministry among our young people, but one that is not nearly as attractive.

Until a leadership knows which previously mentioned target they would choose, were they given only these two targets as choices, double-mindedness will prevail. The problem of modernity is real and must be addressed. In other words, people in our times expect and demand that their felt needs be met. The leadership of the church must resist the temptation to cave in to every demand under the threat of departure. Yet to neglect the felt needs of people can also cause the church to be irrelevant in the modern world.

So let me say it once again: To choose to meet the unfelt needs of church attenders and members as a priority over their wants is not to choose that the church will grow more slowly. *But it may.* I've said through the years that if we at Perimeter wanted merely to have a large church, unconcerned about the maturity of its people, we would have made many decisions differently than we did. But be careful. Don't use quality as an excuse for not growing. Healthy churches, when located in high harvest areas, *will* grow.

WHAT IS INEVITABLE

If you are a pastor who is passionate about leading a prevailing church, get ready for criticism. Many in the laity will not understand all that has been said above. They will come to you with what appears to them to be the obvious answers to all concerns—but they don't understand the implications of their choices. We must. Thus, every decision regarding choice of values necessitates much prayer and counsel. Then we must stick to our guns as long as we believe we've made the best choice for the church. At the same time, we must humbly admit it when we realize we've made a bad choice in our position on a continuum.

When my life comes to an end, or if the Lord returns while I'm still alive, I want to know that I have been faithful in my discharge of duties as a pastor of His church. When that day comes, nothing else will matter—not the size of the church I pastor or any other human measurement of success. Until then, giving glory to God by making His bride as beautiful as she can be must remain my passion—and the passion of every other church leader. To that end and only to that end must we be satisfied. And such beauty will be greatly enhanced, as the church becomes more and more committed to and proficient in evangelism and discipleship. In the next two chapters I will explain why I feel so strongly about this.

NOTE

1. Adapted from James C. Collins and Jerry I. Porras, *Built to Last* (New York: HarperCollins, 1994, 1997), 202.

Chapter Twenty

Strategies
for Evangelism

As I noted in the last chapter, this chapter and the next deal with the two passions that underlie everything else in this book. Whether we look at the Great Commission in Matthew 28:18–20 or Jesus' restatement of His command in Acts 1:8, the call to passionate evangelism and discipleship is unmistakable. Evangelism and discipleship are the squeaky wheels of the effective ministry plan. They must be greased. Without biblical evangelism and discipleship, a ministry plan is doomed to ultimate failure. The plan may look good on paper and even produce a flurry of activity, but it will not lead to a prevailing church.

Evangelism and discipleship are unavoidably linked in the life of a healthy church. Disciples evangelize as an evidence of effective discipleship. Discipleship without evangelism represents purposeless spiritual intake. Jesus did not picture the reality of spiritual life by describing us as reservoirs into which He would pour His life and Spirit. He talked about giving us living water that wells up, flows out, and passes on to others (John 4). Until the gospel begins to leak out of us, we haven't fully received it.

INDIVIDUAL EQUIPPING

I believe that every church should have a plan and at least one method for equipping believers to individually share their faith. To simply expect church members to be "bringers" to church in order to let the professionals do the evangelism is to rob them of their privilege and responsibility to be soul winners. Certainly all do not have the spiritual gifts and natural abilities to make them abundantly fruitful in evangelism. Christians who do not have the gifts of giving or mercy are still expected to give and show mercy. So too, all Christians can share their faith with the lost. Their approaches will differ and their fruitfulness will vary, but all can share the good news of Christ. It is the church leadership's responsibility to make certain that such equipping is made available.

As they are adequately equipped and challenged to identify, pray for, and relationally invest in a target group (a list of individuals or an identifiable group such as a neighborhood, apartment complex, or social club), increased fruitfulness should be expected.

We have a course at Perimeter called X-PRESS Your Faith that is offered five times a year. It is here (as well as in discipleship teams) that our people can get equipped to witness.

X-PRESS summarizes and implements what we expect of our people. We explain that the X is actually the letter of the Greek alphabet named *chi*. It is the first letter of the Greek word *Christou*, which means Christ. We want to remind them that Christ must always be out front. Then the acronym PRESS stands for *Pray*, *Relate*, *Expose*, *Share*, and *Sponsor*. During the equipping sessions we help prepare our people to do all five.

EIGHT SUGGESTIONS FOR EFFECTIVELY REACHING THE LOST

Perimeter has developed a specific plan and methodology for evangelism training that has stood the test of time. Many pastors and leaders have been trained in our seminars and have repeatedly asked us to make our curriculum more readily accessible. We will soon be making those materials available in printed form. In the meantime, let me make eight suggestions for pastors who want to see their churches used effectively to reach the lost. These are in addition to the obvious requirement of demonstrating lifestyles of mercy intent on meeting the needs of hurting people who don't grasp the love of Christ. I feel these suggestions will at least give you a framework from which to think about the role of evangelism in the life of your church.

1. Lead your elder leadership (or its equivalent) to embrace a philosophy of ministry which makes reaching the lost as high a priority as ministering to God's people.

I can't stress strongly enough the importance of casting the vision well and often for the value of reaching the lost. Both in elder training and in elder orientation, I underscore this value as dramatically as possible. But most importantly, they must see their pastor living out a passion for the lost.

2. Indoctrinate your people through multiple ongoing means as to the high value your church places on reaching the lost.

My "best shot" at this is during what we call our "Inquirer's Seminar," required of all people who would choose to join the church. This is a weekend seminar where they can learn about Perimeter. If, after the weekend, they choose to join, they can attend our Membership Seminar and then meet with elders to be examined for membership. This first seminar is my opportunity to indelibly imprint their minds with the high value of being part of a mission-minded church. The seminar introduces the newcomer to what we call "The Three Distinctives of Perimeter Church." One of our three distinctives has to do with being an effective mission that remains contemporary to its culture. The other two include being a safe home that meets the needs of God's people and being an effective equipping station that views the pastor and staff as equippers and the laity as the ministers. During the seminar I want to sell our newcomers on the high value we place on reaching the lost.

Sermons, vision banquets, newsletters, and statement of vision and mission must continuously remind the newcomers and old-timers alike that reaching the lost is a nonnegotiable commitment of the church.

3. Make your church services and ministries seeker friendly.

I have already addressed the importance of making the worship service friendly to nonbelievers. But the same should be applied to all ministries of the church. It is important to evaluate everything in the life of the church, from its name to its recreational ministry, to determine whether it is not only friendly to the lost, but, in fact, strategically designed to reach the lost. Until you have done this, you have not applied the principle of alignment to the church.

When we began our church it was named Perimeter Presbyterian Church, based on the commitment we had and have to plant God's church all around and throughout the Perimeter (the name given to an interstate highway that encircles Atlanta). As we began to take seriously our commitment to reach the unchurched, we inventoried everything we could think of regarding how we were postured to reach the lost.

When we looked at our name, we concluded that in our particular community, *Presbyterian* did not serve well in reaching the lost—only in attracting Presbyterians. Right or wrong in our evaluation, based on our belief, we changed our name to Perimeter Church—all for the sake of eliminating barriers to reaching the lost.

4. Teach your people to answer the questions that nonbelievers are asking.

One of the leading reasons that faithful believers struggle to share their faith has to do with their fear of not being able to answer the questions that nonbelievers are asking. To eliminate such fear, we must teach our people the answers to the most commonly asked questions.

Three such questions are:

> ◄ *How can Christians believe that the Bible is God's Word and without error? Isn't it somewhat naïve to believe such?*

❧ *How can Christians believe that all people, including moral and religious people outside of Christianity, deserve eternal punishment? Isn't such a belief an overstatement?*

❧ *How can Christians believe that of all the religious leaders throughout time, Jesus is the only way to God? Isn't that a bit narrow?*

There is a fourth question that does not raise the seeker's curiosity as much as the previous three, yet is equally important.

❧ *According to the Bible, how does a person gain eternal life?*

We have discovered that putting these answers in four booklets has been a confidence booster to our people. Though during our training we require the trainees to learn the answers, these four booklets, entitled *Life Issue*, are each coupled with five chapters of the gospel of John, (except the fourth booklet, which has the final six chapters). These serve well to help the seeker in a week-to-week investigation.

5. *Teach your people how to wisely create a forum to address the questions that nonbelievers are asking—preferably, by teaching them how to have multiple appointment conversations rather than to make single appointment presentations.*

For many years I presented the gospel to nonbelievers primarily using a tract. Then I graduated, so to speak, to monologuing the gospel (explaining the gospel in a single presentation). But that was years ago. I was still living among people who primarily had backgrounds that prepared them to embrace the values and even the beliefs of Christianity. I found that a monologue presentation of the gospel was sufficient. But as society has become more and more secularized, monologuing the gospel is most often inadequate. I found that after I presented the gospel and asked a person if they would consider accepting Christ, the seekers would often decline, suggesting that they didn't agree with my views regarding the Bible, lost people, or Christ. I felt much like Barney Fyfe with his one bullet in his front pocket. I would load my bullet, take aim, shoot, strike my target between the eyes, only to see him charging me— and I was out of ammunition!

It was at this time that I discovered the advantage of dialoguing the gospel. My theology has always underscored the reality that God does the converting using His converting tool, the Bible. I have believed for years that I can never change the heart of a person dead in his sin. Now for the first time I began to see my beliefs fleshed out as God used multiple appointments in which I dialogued the gospel to change hearts.

Untold numbers of times I have seen a nonbeliever who was in total disagreement with the gospel become a faithful follower after only a few weeks of investigation.

We have developed of a simple diagram that can be used to stimulate an appetite to investigate Christianity. It helps the believer and invites the unbeliever to recognize that their questions and objections to Christianity are actually quite common and can be clearly answered from Scripture. We train our people to use that tool to create a forum for such an investigation.

However, the particular method chosen is not nearly as important as is the existence of a specific method (or methods) with which church members can be adequately equipped.

6. *Model for your congregation a lifestyle of being faithful as an evangelist, humbly telling your personal stories of opportunities to share your faith.*

As the saying goes, "more is caught than taught." If we as pastors are not sharing our faith on a day-to-day basis, neither will many of our people. If we don't share stories of our evangelistic encounters (including the failures), they will not "catch" the mission or be encouraged by our example. Hearing stories of leading people to Christ is not as important as hearing stories of faithfulness in sharing the gospel (regardless of the outcome).

7. Create periodic churchwide, culturally relevant outreach events for the sake of providing easy opportunities for your people to invite unchurched friends.

In addition to the obvious advantages to such events, there is a not so obvious benefit that comes as a by-product—a healthy self-esteem as a church experiencing firsthand the reality of being a church that is relevant to the unchurched. The more the people see their church as mission oriented, the more they will see themselves as contributors to the cause.

8. Create a discipleship-oriented small-group ministry that equips your people to share their faith, holds them accountable to do so, and uses a group approach to reach the unchurched (which allows the participants to focus on their spiritual gifts to directly contribute to reaching the lost).

One of the subjects that cannot be neglected in the curriculum used to equip church members is that of disciple making. As mentioned earlier, there is no better forum for equipping and holding disciples accountable than in a small-group setting.

As a small group shares in prayer for each other's target list and perhaps even shares in relational and outreach endeavors to reach a common target group, each individual can celebrate the conversion of the lost, regardless of who actually communicated the gospel story.

Since I have used the term *target group* several times, let me explain what I mean by those words. It is a term we use to refer to a people group for which you pray and with which you invest discretionary time—all for the sake of introducing them to Christ and His kingdom.

Tennis Evangelism

After moving to Atlanta, I discovered that 60,000 Atlantans were on tennis teams organized around neighborhoods, social clubs, and apartment complexes. I decided to take up tennis, in part to have a common ground with non-Christians.

After playing tennis for a few years and having targeted the tennis community as my target group, I was offered an unusual gift by a close friend in our church who was being transferred to another city. He told me he wanted to give me a present as an expression of his appreciation for the ministry our church had had with him and his family. He then said, "I want to give you a gift of prayer." I had no idea what he meant by this. He explained that he would commit to pray faithfully for me for anything I asked—given four conditions.

First, it must be something I wanted and didn't need. Second, I must be willing to pray with him for this request. Third, it must be something I believed only God could provide. And last, we must agree to tell no one we were praying for this request so as not to engineer our own answer to prayer.

Without much thought, I responded with a genuine but "impossible" request. I asked for a membership to a very nice indoor/outdoor tennis club less than a mile from where our church facilities were being built. I knew I couldn't afford a membership to this club and if I could, people would be critical of my ability to do so as a pastor. But I knew that if given as a gift no shadow could be cast.

Within a week or so, a man in our church who was in the latter stages of a battle with cancer contacted me and explained that he had previously arranged the sale of his membership to this same club and while negotiating the sale had had the idea of transferring the membership to my name, without cost to me. He asked me if I would be interested in such a gift. I immediately asked if he was aware of our prayers for such a gift. He was not. He was thrilled to find himself a part of something God was doing.

It was not long after this that I was asked by a friend if I had met the head teaching pro of the club. I had not, but knew who he was by sight. My friend encouraged me to get with this pro, suggesting that he was in great need of faith in Christ.

By the providence of God, within a week or so, we parked next to each other at the same time at the tennis complex. I introduced myself to him (but certainly not telling him I was a pastor) and suggested we hit some tennis balls or have lunch together some time soon. His response was, "That would be great, but what I would really like to do is to get into one of your men's early morning Bible study groups I've heard about." I was shocked. I asked if he knew I was a pastor. He responded by saying, "Sure, everyone around here knows that a preacher has joined the club!"

I suggested that instead of getting into one of my existing groups, that we start one at the club. He agreed to host it, secure a room, provide breakfast and mail invitations to his buddies at the club whom he thought, as himself, needed to attend a Bible study. Within a few weeks the study began with a healthy attendance. Now, nearly twenty years later, that study still continues and there is no telling how many people have come to Christ over the years through this ministry.

God honors the intent to identify a target group and then to pray for it and to invest in it. I've witnessed this at Perimeter and in many other churches.

Unusual Targets

I heard one pastor share the story of challenging his church members to identify a target group. When he was through speaking, a young mother came up to him and enthusiastically announced that she had identified her target group. He asked her what it was.

Her reply: "Young mothers who are potty training their children."

He wanted to laugh, but resisted only because of reading the seriousness written on her face. He asked how she planned to do this.

She immediately answered, "I plan to reserve the community room at the local library, and then put up posters around the community advertising a class on potty training. I will then get a lady in our church who has successfully potty trained her own children to teach the class—asking her to include sharing how her faith became an asset to her."

Not only was this first meeting successful, the pastor said, but because of demand it was made a permanent course. Over time, special elective classes were offered geared toward specialty needs such as potty training twins, potty training the strong-willed child, and so on. (Basically, they started a potty training university!) After a few years, this ministry had been responsible for over two hundred women becoming Christians.

SENDING OUT EVANGELISTS

The apostle Peter, writing to believers in general, offered a helpful word of direction that more Christians need to take to heart. He based his counsel on the assumption that the lives of believers would be so marked by hope that others would feel compelled to ask questions. He wrote, "But in your hearts set apart Christ as Lord. Always be prepared to give an answer to everyone who asks you to give the reason for the hope that you have. But do this with gentleness and respect" (1 Peter 3:15 NIV). First, he established the motivation for evangelism—discipleship. Disciples who set apart Christ as Lord in their hearts. Then, he outlines a question that every believer should have to answer on a regular basis: "In what ways have you prepared to give an answer to everyone who asks?" Evangelism doesn't happen off-the-cuff. Effective evangelism—what appears to be effortless sharing of one's faith—is really the product of specific preparation and openness to the leading of God's Spirit. Peter's question remains an unavoidable and haunting point of accountability: "What are you prepared to say if someone asks you about your hope this week?"

Discipleship prepares us to share hope with others. Discipleship training is the other core ingredient of the kind of believers that a prevailing church produces. Discipleship will be our focus in the next and final chapter.

———∞∞∞———

Chapter Twenty-One

A Case for Two
Sides of Discipleship

D iscipleship training (discipleship) is, for the most part, a lost practice in churches today. I realize that the word *discipleship* is used in many ways and that there are many varieties (or degrees) of discipleship. But as I speak of discipleship here, I refer to the most mature form defined as *life-on-life, laboring in the lives of a few*.

As I noted in the last chapter, the link between discipleship and evangelism must be recognized and addressed. Evangelism and discipleship are the food and drink of the prevailing church. Healthy survival depends on a consistent practice of biblical evangelism (providing the means for people to respond in faith to Christ) and discipleship (providing the specific means for people to grow in their faith, including becoming equipped to share that faith with others). Although a full treatment of discipleship is beyond the scope of this book, I would like to at least provide what I hope is a compelling case for a thoughtful, persistent, planned approach to discipleship in the local church.

DISCIPLESHIP IMPERATIVE

The need for such discipleship becomes all too obvious when we consider the following four realities:

1. Every believer has been or is presently living under great bondage to sin.

This reality is taught throughout Scripture. At The Fall, man lost his moral ability (not his natural ability). This means that though he can do the right things, he has no ability to do the right things for the right reasons. Thus we understand statements made by Paul in Romans 3 such as "There is none righteous, not even one" (v. 10); "There is none who seeks for God" (v. 11); and "There is none who does good, there is not even one" (v. 12). Everyone is conceived in sin (Psalm 51:5) and remains in bondage to sin until delivered from its power by the redemptive work of Christ applied by the Holy Spirit.

As sinners we are controlled by the influences of three forces: the world, the devil, and the flesh. Paul clearly explains this in Ephesians 2:1–3:

> And you were dead in your trespasses and sins, in which you formerly walked according to the course of this world, according to the prince of the power of the air, of the spirit that is now working in the sons of disobedience. Among them we too all formerly lived in the lusts of our flesh, indulging the desires of the flesh and of the mind, and were by nature children of wrath, even as the rest.

Paul's words to describe "in bondage to sin" are "dead in your trespasses and sins" (v. 1). In verse 2, Paul describes the cause for this first by using the phrase, "course of this world." *Course* refers to a controlling influence, and *world* suggests a view of life without God. Thus "course of this world" refers to a world and life view that discounts God's presence and purpose in the world.

The second influence leading to bondage to sin is described in verse 2 as "the prince of the power of the air." *Air* refers to "unseen power." This one, otherwise known as Satan, is "working in the sons of disobedience." This term *working* carries the idea of energy, force, or power. No wonder the non-Christian is in bondage to sin!

The last influence mentioned is referred to as "the flesh." There are four common uses of the term *flesh* in Scripture. Two of them are used in verse two. The first usage refers to that which is opposite of "spirit," and the second usage refers to the animal part of man. The second usage describes the "flesh's" dominion as "living in the lusts [cravings] of the flesh." As long as we remained nonbelievers, our cravings determined our actions. These may have been good desires in and of themselves, but they were not under our full control (i.e., hunger, thirst, pleasure, sex, the desire to attract).

The second example of the flesh control is described as "indulging the desires of the mind," referring to the emotional and intellectual part of man. In other words, our minds are fallen too. Those characteristics that control man's thoughts in this condition are the likes of pride, hate, and ambition.

I think it is safe to conclude that man in his sinful condition is in a most desperate predicament. Thus, we are not surprised at Paul's concluding description of such a sinner as "by nature, children of wrath." Not a pretty picture.

On or Off the Wagon

Using this biblical picture as a backdrop, imagine with me that you have a close friend who you are convinced is an alcoholic. He (or she) is acting unusually irresponsible and developing patterns of avoidance. In an effort to help your friend, you confront him about his abuse of alcohol. To your surprise he admits for the first time that he is addicted to alcohol. He agrees that his addiction is going to cause him to hurt not only himself but those closest to him. He then tells you in all sincerity that he is committed from this moment on to never drink again.

Now suppose you had to bet all the money you have on whether he would stop drinking. Regardless of how sincere you believe him to be, you know good and well that he will almost certainly start drinking (probably sooner than later).

So, what counsel would you give him? I would imagine that you would do everything in your power to urge him to check into a treatment center to get "dried out."

Now, suppose he stays in such a center for several weeks and comes out excited to find himself no longer even desiring a drink. Assume you have to bet all your money once again as to whether he would stay dry. I would imagine that you would have to put your money on the probability of a relapse. Though you would have hope for your friend's continued recovery, based on statistics you would still have little confidence in long-term sobriety.

So, what would you counsel your friend now? I suspect you would encourage him to begin attending Alcoholics Anonymous meetings (or some equivalent). Once this pattern of responsible behavior becomes routine, you now have a real dilemma as to how to bet your money.

Addicted to Sin

Much like this alcoholic, all humans are addicted to sin. Not until one admits to such is there hope for deliverance. But even then one must get "dried out." Scripture refers to this as regeneration or the work of God's Spirit giving a person a new heart. Only then is he freed from the controlling power of sin. This leads to the second reality.

2. Decisions to leave sin addictions are routinely followed by relapses.

Just as alcoholics have a tendency to relapse, so do believers. There is a saying in AA, "Once an alcoholic, always an alcoholic." Likewise, believers must admit "once a sinner, always a sinner" (prior to glorification). Common relapses for believers include worry, bitterness, selfishness, misplaced priorities, idolatry, sexual disobedience, poor stewardship, and the list goes on and on.

Spiritual Relapses

From September through June I meet weekly with my Discipleship Team. We meet only monthly during July and August. During a mid-summer meeting, I asked the guys, "Using 98.6 Fahrenheit as a standard, what was your spiritual temperature the day our group stopped meeting weekly?" All indicated a very healthy reading—typically only a few tenths of a degree off the desired temperature. Then I asked, "What is your reading right now?" All but one reported a worse reading than one month previously. Certainly this says a lot about the value of being in a small group, but also illustrates the tendency to relapse into old sinful addictions. A third reality introduces us to the solution to such common relapses.

3. *Life-on-life, laboring in the lives of a few, is God's master plan for rescuing addicts.*

Ask any recovering alcoholic how they got out of their addiction and they will say, "It took a sponsor to get me where I am."

Management guru Peter Drucker has said that in his opinion AA is one of only two social institutions in the world today that are working. Why is that? It is primarily because of their use of sponsors. Those in recovery are encouraged to find a sponsor as soon as possible, to provide life-on-life accountability as the alcoholic works through the twelve steps. During that process, they are also encouraged to make themselves available to sponsor a recent survivor.

Recovering Sinners

Likewise, with those who have experienced redemption, success in sustaining freedom from sin addictions goes up significantly when a spiritual sponsor (or discipler) is available.

Jesus certainly modeled sponsorship. He made a significant investment in the lives of twelve men and an even deeper one in the lives of three. The New Testament describes such an investment relationally in younger believers on numerous occasions. For instance, the apostle Paul said in

2 Timothy 2:2 (NASB 1977, italics added), "And the things which you have heard from me in the presence of many witnesses, *these entrust* to faithful men, who will be able to teach others also." He also told his brothers and sisters in Corinth, "Now these things, brethren, I have figuratively applied to myself and Apollos for your sakes, that *in us* you might learn not to exceed what is written, in order that no one of you might become arrogant in behalf of one against the other" (1 Corinthians 4:6 NASB 1977, italics added). In 1 Thessalonians 2:8 (NASB 1977, italics added), Paul revealed the secret to effective ministry when he wrote, "Having thus a fond affection for you, we were well-pleased *to impart to you* not only the gospel of God but *also our own lives*, because you had become very dear to us."

Life Product

I define such discipleship as "having a life product, being intentional about imparting that life product, and doing the right things to impart that life product (truth, equipping, accountability, mission, and supplication)." It is as we've described it, "life-on-life, laboring in the lives of a few."

I recently asked an AA participant how they got enough sponsors. His response was immediate. He said, "When you've lived in the grip of alcoholism, you know its destructiveness. You also know that you would never have been delivered from its grip without the help of a sponsor. Once you've been delivered, you can't help but want to help others experience the same freedom." It's unfortunate that many believers do not use the same line of reasoning about discipling new and immature believers struggling to find freedom from sin addictions.

This same friend shared that there is also a selfish motivation for sponsoring others. He said, "We have a saying in AA that goes like this: 'You can't keep it without giving it away.'" I'm convinced the same is true regarding deliverance from sin. This leads to a final reality.

4. *Without life-on-life discipleship, we run the risk of producing immature believers, at best, and disillusioned learners, at worst.*

As mentioned in chapter 9, Ken Blanchard's book *Leadership and the One Minute Manager: Increasing Effectiveness Through Situational Leadership* helps us to understand that going directly from directives to delegation creates disillusioned learners. If coaching and support are never provided or if they are removed, the hope of healthy development is minimized significantly.

Pastors and church leaders have to choose between two goals. The first is to see their people grow in knowledge and commitment. Most leaders would be thrilled to reach this goal. But further thought causes one to realize that this falls far short of the ideal. The second goal is to see people grow in maturity and equipping.

Though the second goal of maturity and equipping is inclusive of the first (knowledge and commitment), the reverse cannot be said. The reality is that knowledge and commitment alone do not take people out of moral addictions and mental and emotional bondage. Only maturity accomplishes this. And maturity is hard to come by without the investment of a sponsor or discipler.

The church must take seriously the requirement of life-on-life, laboring in the lives of a few. The leadership of churches must begin to consider how to equip their people to be effective disciplers. In order for discipleship to be extremely effective, it must demonstrate a balance between being *organic* and *engineered*. To this end, we must understand the two sides of discipleship.

ORGANIC DISCIPLESHIP

Organic discipleship describes the *life-on-life* side of discipleship. It is Jesus saying to His disciples, "Follow Me." This is the "caught" part of discipleship in comparison with the "taught" part. It is being together, learning with the world's circumstances as the classroom and the discipler's life and experiences as the textbook (all based on the foundation of the Word of God). Such discipleship may take place on the basketball court or going together on an evangelistic appointment. This is relationship over a period of time long enough to involve significant life challenges for both the disciple and the discipler.

ENGINEERED DISCIPLESHIP

Engineered discipleship is a term used to describe the structural and planned side of discipleship. This is the intentional teaching side of discipleship. God's Word also provides the basis for content. In organic discipleship, God's Word provides answers, responses, and guidance in immediate situations; in engineered discipleship, God's Word provides preparation, instruction, and equipping for yet-to-be-faced challenges in life. Decisions must be wisely made as to what truths will be taught and how equipping will take place.

DISCIPLESHIP CURRICULUM

Some today view any curriculum used in discipleship as anathema. Most who hold to such a perspective see curriculum as a detractor from being organic (life-on-life). Certainly, this could be the case. But it doesn't have to be. Using the same logic that Jesus applied when He said, "If your right hand offends you, cut it off" (Matthew 5:30 paraphrased), I too would agree that if the use of a curriculum means one will not labor life-on-life then that curriculum should not be used. But how much better to have the hand not be offensive. It is much better to have life-on-life discipleship while using an excellent curriculum. The disciples walked with Jesus and observed Him day by day. But the Scriptures are also clear that He taught them content, challenged their thinking, and explained parables. Everything His Father told Him was Jesus' curriculum (see John 7:16; 14:10, 24).

My logic is as follows. If I can only spend one time a week for two or three years meeting with a small group of guys in discipleship, I want to make sure every minute counts. I can either randomly choose what I will teach, let the guys in my group determine what I will teach, or be thoughtful and selective in what I teach. All three possibilities end up becoming a curriculum. However, I have found the latter approach to have the highest likelihood of being the best.

I began designing a curriculum for my use in discipleship by writing down everything that came to my mind which I thought my guys needed to know in order to live for Christ as mature and equipped followers of Christ. I then eliminated what was least important in order to have a reasonable amount of information to digest in the allotted time we would be together.

When I was in college, I challenged a handful of guys each year to be discipled. I invited them to join a group where I would labor in their lives to take them to a more faithful and mature walk with Christ. I would carefully lay out the cost explaining that we would meet three times a week for the entire school year. Once a week we would meet to study the Word of God and to discuss the things studied as assignments during the previous week. We would meet once a week to do evangelism together (sharing our faith in a selected men's dorm). The third meeting each week was for the purpose of socializing together. So, every week I spent one night in a setting well suited for the engineered side of discipleship and two times a week for the organic side.

When I moved to Atlanta to plant a church, I immediately began the same procedure. I remember asking my first potential disciple if he would be interested in being discipled. He responded enthusiastically in the affirmative. I then asked when was a good time to meet. He mentioned that an early morning day of the week, prior to work, would be best.

I responded saying, "Great! When else?"

He looked at me like a deer caught in headlights and cautiously asked, "What do you mean, when else?"

I explained that I needed three times a week. He answered by asking me the following series of questions:

❧ *Do you know that I work fifty to sixty hours a week?*

❧ *Do you know that I have a wife and three kids?*

❧ *Do you know that I travel several nights a week?*

❧ *Do you know that I have a house and a yard to keep up on the weekends?*

❧ *What do you mean three times a week?*

I realized in that moment that the real world of an adult was much different than life as a student. And likewise, it was then that I concluded that discipleship would be much more difficult in the modern American adult world.

I have had to adapt my approach to discipleship, without compromising my values and priorities. As a contrast to two out of three weekly gatherings being devoted to organic discipleship during my college days, now two-thirds of my once-a-week gatherings must be spent devoted to the organic. With only one-third of my time available for the engineered discipleship, I must make every minute count.

Now most of our time together is spent in discussion and equipping regarding what was learned on one's own during the week (as opposed to using the meeting time to teach the information that needed to be learned). Selected biblical texts for personal study and books and tapes become valuable tools to make learning an all-week-long experience and not a once-a-week occasion.

A BALANCED CURRICULUM

A well-thought-through curriculum has proven to be an invaluable addition to my discipleship efforts. However, it can be abused and thus become a disadvantage. A typical signal that a leader is "engineer bound" is the statement, "I can't get through the materials."

In my opinion, a healthy curriculum for discipleship is well-balanced between systematic theology, practical theology, and biblical theology (defined previously in chapter 16). Systematic theology gives the believer a skeletal framework upon which to hang all of his biblical learning for the rest of his or her life. The vast majority of biblical theology should be learned daily in personal devotions and Bible study. I acknowledge that some lobby for making the discipleship gathering primarily a Bible study. Though Bible study is extremely important, the goal of discipling should focus far more on equipping believers with how to study on their own than on studying a few books of the Bible as a group. Don't misunderstand me! Bible study groups are extremely valuable. But discipleship teams are designed for a totally different purpose.

If you are committed to life-on-life, laboring in the lives of a few, be diligent to keep a healthy balance between the organic and engineered functions of discipleship. When Mark described Jesus' choosing of the original twelve disciples, he included a brief statement of purpose: "And He appointed twelve, so that they would be with Him" (Mark 3:14). Yes, He would eventually send them out to preach and give them authority over demons, but first He wanted them to "be with Him." Jesus' commission to His followers at the end of Matthew specifically mentioned disciples as the product of their ministry throughout the world. The prevailing church is made up of mature and equipped disciples of Jesus Christ.

Conclusion

What makes a church grow? I see many churches whose pastors love the Lord and have an exceptional prayer life. The singular, focused cause of these churches seems to be the glory of God; their theology and teaching gifts are exceptional; they are in communities that give evidence of being "ripe unto harvest." Yet for some reason these churches fail to effectively reap that harvest. Time and again the evidence is that this fruitlessness is linked to a failure to develop and implement an effective ministry plan.

Yet, even so, a prevailing church is the by-product of the power of the gospel, not of outstanding ministry planning. But the two should never be seen to be mutually exclusive of one another. Every aspect of a ministry plan must be driven by the gospel. Every plan and decision should be made so as to better proclaim and live out the gospel.

No aspect of what the church does is going to result in people transformation or community transformation outside the work of the gospel. The gospel, the good news of Christ's work on our behalf, must not only be the focus of the church, but also its power (Romans 1:16).

Outside this understanding, church ministry becomes nothing more than perfecting technique and programs. The focus shifts from what God does to what man does. Man can create large, growing, and popular churches, but only God can create churches that bring a community into a life-changing encounter with the kingdom of God. A ministry plan designed with a focus on and a dependence upon the gospel will make the heart more excited about God's broader kingdom than will simply the size and perceived success of the local church itself. What God does in the community through the church will be celebrated more than the size of its weekend attendance or its budget.

Only when the good news is understood and embraced for what it is will the church become what God intends it to be—a prevailing church.

Some of my closest theological peers may well see this book as a "how to" book of practical steps to making a great church. That couldn't be further from the truth. I don't deny the value of practical and wise advice (in fact, I believe such is important), but only the work of God, by the work of His Spirit, can make a church prevail.

I once heard someone say that a church must function well as a *cause*, a *community*, and a *corporation* (organization), and that few pastors are gifted to excel in leading their churches well in all three. This book is written with a special interest in helping those who perhaps love to advance the cause of Christ by pastoring, preaching, and teaching, and thrive on building biblical community among God's people, but who find the organizational issues of ministry a distraction and a challenge. It is my hope that all will see how excellence in the "corporational" issues of churches can magnify the strengths of their cause and their community.

God's church, embracing its rightful confession of Christ, is the one weapon against which the gates of hades cannot prevail. So let's give ourselves to the church, for the glory of God, so as to see His kingdom come on this earth even as it is in heaven.

Appendix

The ten components that make up an effective ministry plan are listed below, along with the key question that must be answered in order to ensure that component has been included.

Component 1: A God-Honoring Purpose
    Question: Why do we exist?

Component 2: A Faith-Oriented Commitment
    Question: In what ways will we demonstrate a faith commitment?

Component 3: A God-Given Vision
    Question: What are we seeking to accomplish?

Component 4: Well-Prioritized Values
Question: What is most important to us?

Component 5: A Well-Defined Mission
Question: How do we plan to accomplish our vision?

Component 6: Biblically Based Job Descriptions
Question: Who is responsible for what in accomplishing the vision?

Component 7: A Strategically Defined Infrastructure
Question: How will we structure our organization so as to accomplish our mission?

Component 8: A Culturally Oriented Strategy
Question: How will we accomplish our mission?

Component 9: Well-Documented Goals
Question: How will we know that we are accomplishing our mission and vision?

Component 10: A Time-Bound Schedule
Question: What is a reasonable time line of specific tasks that must take place in order to accomplish our goals?